Compelling Knowledge

Compelling Knowledge

A Feminist Proposal
for an
Epistemology of the Cross

Mary M. Solberg

STATE UNIVERSITY OF NEW YORK PRESS

Published by
State University of New York Press, Albany

© *1997 State University of New York*

*For information, address the State University of New York Press
State University Plaza, Albany, NY 12246*

*Production by Dana Foote
Marketing by Dana E. Yanulavich*

Library of Congress Cataloging-in-Publication Data

Solberg, Mary M., 1947–
    Compelling knowledge : a feminist proposal for an epistemology of
the Cross / Mary M. Solberg.
        p.   cm.
    Includes bibliographical references and index.
    ISBN 0-7914-3379-X (alk. paper). — ISBN 0-7914-3380-3 (pbk. :
alk. paper)
    1. Christian ethics.   2. Feminist ethics.   3. Knowledge, Theory of
(Religion)   4. Jesus Christ—Crucifixion.   5. Atonement.
6. Liberation theology.   7. El Salvador—History—1979–1992.   8. El
Salvador—History—Religious aspects—Christianity.   9. Solberg,
Mary M., 1947– . I. Title.
BJ1278.F45S64   1997
241'.082—dc21   96–40119
                                                                          CIP

10 9 8 7 6 5 4 3 2 1

This book is dedicated to the poor
of El Salvador, who both are and
represent those friends of Jesus,
nearby and far away, to whom I must
account for my theologizing;
and to Sonia.

Contents

vii

Preface: A Meditation on El Salvador

For almost three years (1983–86) I lived and worked with the church in El Salvador, which was then in the midst of a prolonged and brutal civil war.

That experience brought me face to face with a reality that had never been *real* to me before. Of course I knew that people suffered, that poverty and war existed, that life was very difficult for some. But this was knowing of the formal sort: information. Being there, living there, going to sleep and waking up there, breathing that air and smelling that dust, listening to the people speak, bore down on me in my own flesh (in Spanish, *en carne propia*), and I began to apprehend how things were in a way I had not been able—or perhaps willing—to acknowledge before. I could no longer turn away and willfully or unwittingly plead ignorance. Disembodied knowledge became embodied.

Both the fact and the manner of this knowing implicated me at first hand. I could not lay off my accountability. I could not have evaded it, quite apart from my status as a white and privileged North American; as a fellow human being, I felt answerable to those who suffered. As I reflected on the nature of that special status—captured with exquisite irony in the fact that I had chosen to accept an invitation to arrive in El Salvador in the first place, and could leave whenever I wanted to—my accountability deepened irrevocably. In a host of intertwined ways, I was answerable, both *for* the suffering whose reality I could no longer shut out or explain away, and *to* those whose lives "suffering" described.

The challenge to one who would preach the gospel in places like El Salvador, I heard Jon Sobrino say, was how to proclaim God's love to those whom poverty and fear are killing. For me, the challenge was *how to live*, knowing of such suffering and of my implication in it. How to live, indeed? No wonder we "don't know" about the suffering of the poor, the excluded, the marginalized— far from us and next door. Who *wants* to know such realities? Who can live with such knowledge, especially coupled with recognition of complicity by acts of omission or of commission?

My first response to the reality into which my life was being stitched was to try to "fix" what was wrong: in acts of concrete assistance, to try to reverse individual situations of suffering caused by impoverishment, violence, fear, hunger, imprisonment, powerlessness. What came home to me was that as well-intentioned, as needful, as appropriate as these acts were under the circumstances, my attempts to fix what was wrong were, in the face of what *was* wrong, woefully inadequate. If they were laudable as works of charity, they also betrayed my incapacity or refusal to apprehend the depth and breadth and intensity of what was wrong and of the reach of its consequences. In a very important sense, these works could not and did not do what I intended them to do. Moreover, insofar as this brand of "do-ism" kept me busy, it also kept me from seeing, knowing, and acknowledging the extent to which I could not fix what was wrong.

It did not occur to me (then, nor does it now) to argue or to concede that the circumstances simply illustrated human beings' constitutional incapacity to do good, or to alleviate suffering, or to prevent destruction of dignity and lives. This was not for me an occasion to resolve the debate about whether human nature is fundamentally broken and "in bondage to sin," or whether it is fundamentally oriented toward God and able with help from God to do the good. In real life, the matter was much simpler: to see the suffering, and to acknowledge my implication in it. And much more difficult: to find a way to live, knowing what I knew—without excuses, epistemological, anthropological, or ethical.

The fact was that the people whose reality I had been caught up in *were* living—and sometimes dying—knowing suffering, immediately, carnally ("in their own flesh"). In their struggle to be alive, to live with dignity, to protect those they loved, to defeat the evil that threatened to suffocate them, they lived out what I came to see was "hope against hope." They invited me into their homes and opened their hearts. They spoke with plain conviction and faith that undergirded their hope. They taught me that it is possible to see and know—and even live—what *is* the case, even when suffering is the case, and—knowing—to live faithfully as a responsible and responsive Christian. I wondered where I had been before.

For some years now I have been searching for the logic that connects what happened to me in El Salvador and what I am to do here and now. The experience I had there occasioned a profound change, a turning point. I knew even while I was there that what I was experiencing was somehow different from anything I had experienced before. That it would be a turning point, I learned only after the fact.

During my stay there I told visitors from the United States that I felt I had been "humbled," my stiff Norwegian neck had been bowed. Beyond the fact that I could not fix what was wrong, I realized that what was happening around me (and because of that, within me) was not something I could make intellectual sense of. Even copious information and astute analysis were powerless to explicate the meaning of the suffering, or the hope, of those whose struggle for life and dignity was the reason I was there. I also realized that, unaided and exposed, my heart was more likely to break than to make emotional sense of this novel reality.

Nevertheless, what was going on did make sense: deep, embodied, life-giving sense.

When I left El Salvador I knew that, once "home" in the United States, I had to try to understand and express why and how it made sense—and to see whether what had made sense "there" also made sense "here." For the first time, I entered the arena and the language of formal theological reflection, in search of materials and tools that would help me interpret the life-changing events of the previous years.

What was the point of making sense of those events? Beyond the intrinsic fascination and restlessness that fueled my passion for theology, I wanted and needed what I had learned to be of use. It seemed obvious to me that I had been drawn into that very out-of-the-way yet consuming reality for some purpose or purposes: This was part of the sense I sought to make of it. What had happened to me, this as yet unarticulated change, belonged within a larger process of transformation that was occurring as part and result of the struggle to which I had been a witness. Now I was woven into that same struggle, that same commitment.

But in my own place, envisioned and carried out in terms of my own people, my "community of accountability," what was the struggle, the commitment, the point? As I moved from one context to another, I remained accountable to those whose lived witness, with or without their intention, represented to me the reality that I had not been able or willing to see earlier. To live as if they were no longer present, to erase them from my consciousness, would have been both immoral and crazy-making.

I knew that others who had been to El Salvador had had different experiences. Others had seen different things, responded differently. Some saw nothing at all. The temptation, having left, was to imagine that the reality I participated in there was as physically distant and separate from my present location as the remembered experience is from the moment I am now living. The temptation was to return to the safety and insensibility of the "disembodied" knowing with which I began.

Were there, after all, any challenges to take up here?

If my experience in El Salvador is, as I suspect, a parable, a turning point, a catalyst, then what I began to learn there may come to fruition here, too. I know that my theology must respond, and correspond, to this context. My task is not to theologize for the marginalized, but rather for ones like me: white, relatively privileged North American Christians who want to know "what time it is" and, in the face of that reality, how we can live most faithfully.

What have we not known, or not been willing to know? What have we refused to be accountable for, what do we not feel compelled to do because we do not know and are therefore not answerable? Who are those who suffer in our midst, whose suffering we refuse to see, or take account of, because we cannot bear to see it and cannot live with our complicity in it? What can enable us to ask and answer these questions honestly? What sorts and sources of knowing should we consider compelling[1] as we seek to live faithful lives?

There are scores of possible responses to such questions. The particular response that follows is one that issues from what I would call an "epistemological conversion," a transformation of a way of knowing. Such a transformation may draw us to account for our knowing: to see what is the case, acknowledge our implication in it, and recognize ourselves compelled to act on the basis of what we know and how we know ourselves to be answerable.

In any case, this is where the concern emerged: from lived experience, whose authority may be plainer in how we live our lives than it is in any theories about knowing.

> For it is the wisdom of the saints to believe in the truth in opposition to the lie, in the hidden truth in opposition to the manifest truth, and in hope in opposition to hope.[2]

Acknowledgments

Writing is usually difficult and sometimes lonely, but it is hardly ever private. It affects and is affected by a host of people besides the person writing. I would like to acknowledge with thanks some of those who helped: my family, Sonia and Monica Ramírez, who always knew I could do it and were there for the whole thing; my friends—M. B. Walsh, with and from whom I learned so much about theology and feminism; Ann Pederson, who went first and came back for me; Karen Gervais, whose confidence buoyed me over and over; my colleagues at Independence House, Charlie Barber, Alex Bloom, and Larry Riddick, who knew how much this mattered and helped it happen; and my parents, Richard and June Solberg, whose constant love and support continue to show me where I come from.

Union Theological Seminary, where I wrote this book, is a remarkable place, filled with people who have a passion for theology and the difference it ought to make. I am especially grateful to Christopher L. Morse, James H. Cone, Larry Rasmussen, Beverly Wildung Harrison, and Richard Norris, extraordinary teachers—and friends. I am also thankful to Karen Bloomquist, whose willingness to pitch in at the last minute made such a difference.

Most of all, thank God.

Introduction

*Then they also will answer, "Lord,
when was it that we saw you hungry
or thirsty or a stranger or naked
or sick or in prison, and did not take
care of you?"*

(Matthew 25:44, NRSV)

So. Did "they" not see anyone in need? If they did not see, would they have been justified in saying that they did not know anyone was in need? Or did they see, but not know that the one in need was the one they now address as "Lord," revealed in the homeless and the hungry ones? Their question implies that if they had seen, if they had known, they would have done the right thing. They would have acted. They might even have felt compelled to act—if they only had seen "you hungry or thirsty or a stranger or naked or sick or in prison . . . ."

If only they had known.

The Significance of Knowing

People can and do know all sorts of things: about themselves, about the world around them, about God.[1] About their knowing of these things, people claim varying degrees of certainty. To these "knowings," they assign varying degrees of significance, just as they assign varying degrees of value to the objects the knowings are about.

Much that people know matters very little to them. That is to say, people know a great many things that do not make any discernible difference in their day-to-day lives. On one level, such an observation is as unobjectionable as it is obvious. On another level, precisely the lack of correspondence between what people know and what people do often causes great consternation. It especially troubles those who believe that at least some of the time there are powerful reasons for people to mind such discrepancies.

In most cases, of course, what people know has instrumental significance for what they do. Knowing something makes it possible to do something, or to avoid or stop doing something. Scattered across a continuum, people are more or less able, well- or ill-positioned, to make use of all kinds of things they know. When people either fail to act or act inappropriately, others may well associate what they did or did not do with what they knew or did not know (including "know how to do") in this instrumental sense.

Yet another sort of significance people assign to the relationship between knowing and doing appears in the discrepancy between what people know and what they do. People somehow believe or feel or judge that, once they come to know something, what they do ought to be affected by or because of what they know. The "ought" in this case implies that the knowing itself obligates the knower to do something. Ethical significance attaches to knowing that moves a person toward doing commensurate with it.

The line between instrumental and ethical significance may be quite fuzzy, not least because most, if not all, doing is fraught with ethical implications. So, as a matter of fact, is most knowing.

The Ethical Significance of Not-Knowing

It is notoriously difficult to evaluate the relationship between *not*-knowing and doing. "Ignorance is no excuse" has become a cliché largely because it has been said so often to so little effect: usually by those (like police officers) who have lots of evidence that "I didn't know" is frequently and (usually) unapologetically invoked as the excuse for not having done the right thing.

Certainly there is such a thing as understandable, even legitimate, ignorance, the result simply of not having yet been taught or learned what one needs to know. Far more often, though, not-knowing is associated with denial: not being able, or not being willing, to apprehend or to keep in consciousness what is the case. Sometimes, as in the case of traumatic violence, whether domestic abuse or incest, political terror or wartime combat, denial is a means of coping with what the psyche and the heart cannot manage. This sort of necessary, defensive denial itself can damage the personality and well-being of the victim, sometimes irreparably.[2]

Others' denial, their unwillingness to acknowledge, be moved by, and respond to suffering, exacerbates the damage such suffering causes sufferers. Whether human suffering is caused by trauma, or by oppressive practices that grind on and grind up people's lives over decades and centuries, it is too often put out of sight and out of mind. Knowers may work at such ignorance, for it may spare them their own suffering. "When you look at human suffering concretely," Dorothee Sölle observes,

> you destroy all innocence, all neutrality, every attempt to say, "It wasn't I; there was nothing I could do; I didn't know." In the face of suffering you are either with the victim or the executioner— there is no other option . . .[3]

Sacred v. sacred.

Sacred v. Profane.

MATT 25.

3

This sort of unpleasant knowledge inspires another cliché about not-knowing, "Ignorance is bliss." Some, restless with the unwanted sense that they play a part in the suffering around them, feel sorry for or about the sufferers, "but . . . cannot honestly sort out where their own responsibility lies."[4] The not-knowing—guilt-ridden or oblivious—that comes to characterize a whole society feeds into and is nourished by its individual members'—family, friends, neighbors, colleagues, authorities—nonresponses to suffering.

Our resistance to knowing of suffering and of our possible—even likely—complicity in it, extends as far as we need it to: well beyond the bounds of neighborhood and nation. "That we resist the knowledge of our oppression of other peoples," writes Canadian theologian Douglas John Hall, addressing his fellow North Americans,

> is . . . a dimension of the same repressive mind-set which enables us to resist the knowledge of our own subtle oppression. We too are a broken people, covertly broken. Every news broadcast documents our strange, unheralded night.[5]

Even institutions like the communications media and the church, to whom we grant direct access to our homes and our consciences, make little or no effort to put us in the picture or to challenge our not-knowing. Suffering (except of the most spectacular and gruesome sort) is not the type of news multinational corporations' advertising dollars support. Nor is suffering what "church" is about, the gospel notwithstanding.

Despite the stunning examples history furnishes of churches' and societies' awesome capacity for willful ignorance and denial—slavery and the Holocaust are only two such examples—the ethical significance of not-knowing still largely escapes us.

Epistemologies

Philosophers' concerns about knowing, usually collected under the rubric "epistemology,"[6] have focused more often than not on the possibility, the conditions, and the justification of knowledge. Their questions have taken these forms: Is it possible for people to know anything with certainty? How can people be sure—*if* they can be sure—that what they think or believe they know is really the case? How is it possible to show that something known is true, or may be false? These questions express, among other things, the frustration associated with humans' attempt to control their surroundings by naming and knowing. The control those who name and those who know seem to gain over the named and the known resides mainly in the certainty they claim for their knowledge.

Many identify the French philosopher and mathematician René Descartes (1596–1650) as the earliest modern architect of this attempt, which was supposed to lead to what was eventually characterized as "scientific" knowledge and was believed to be the most reliable, the truest. The search for clear and certain epistemological foundations, which took little or no account of historical or cultural assumptions, generated the agendas of some of the finest minds in Western philosophy, including John Locke, George Berkeley, David Hume, Immanuel Kant, Bertrand Russell, A. J. Ayer, and Roderick Chisholm.

Late twentieth-century philosophers of knowledge have benefited from their predecessors' nearly four centuries of hard thinking, which is replete with brilliant insights—and probably some mistakes. Contemporary thinkers, like their predecessors, bear both the weight of the philosophical past and the impress of current events; neither philosophy nor its epistemological subdivision is "an otherwise transcendental science . . . inherently indifferent to human society."[7]

The work of several philosophers, acknowledging the interestedness of philosophy, began to turn over some previously relatively undisturbed epistemological stones. In his 1958 book, *Personal Knowledge*, for example, Michael Polanyi argued that there is no such thing as "impersonal" knowledge; knowing always entails that one make an intensely personal intellectual commitment, shaped by one's vision of reality, which itself evolves, changed by the experiences through which new knowing occurs.[8] More recently, Richard Rorty's *Philosophy and the Mirror of Nature* (1979) argues that the Enlightenment project of foundations and a theory for knowledge was driven by the desire for certainty, rather than wisdom. Questioning whether the mind can ever ground its knowledge in nature, he expresses his skepticism toward "the attempt (which has defined traditional philosophy) to explicate 'rationality' and 'objectivity' in terms of conditions of accurate representation," suggesting that such an attempt is "a self-deceptive effort to eternalize the normal discourse of the day."[9]

Beginning around 1970, distinctively feminist theories of knowledge emerged from a number of sources, largely because

> the conceptual schemes in [the social sciences and biology] and the dominant notions of objectivity, rationality, and scientific method were too weak, or too distorted . . . to be competent even for identifying—let alone eliminating—sexist and androcentric assumptions and beliefs . . . .[10]

Much of the cultural and political clout science possesses resides in its claims to "objective" knowledge. Science has justified those claims on the basis of theories of knowledge that have implicitly or explicitly excluded women as bona fide knowers.[11] Such exclusionary practices and their consequences for science and, more generally, for society, are

FEMINIST EPISTEMOLOGY IS ROOTED IN LIVED EXPERIENCE.

Introduction

Rorty and Polanyi –

rarely acknowledged by those who engage in and benefit from them, even as they continue to claim the epistemological high ground. Feminist critiques, like Rorty's and Polanyi's, wrestle with the personal and interpretive dimensions of knowing, but characteristically they move these issues into the larger social and cultural arena, where conscientious attention to questions about knowers and knowing necessarily includes dealing with political and ethical dimensions.

Feminist epistemologies are deeply rooted in lived experience (particularly that of women), which is significant in several ways. First, while traditional epistemology has often acknowledged and even lifted up "experience" as a necessary component in any account of knowledge, it has generally been understood in the abstract, set next to or over against "reason." Lived experience (the kind real persons have), feminists argue, is always situated: particular and concrete, never abstract nor easily (if at all) universalizable. The impact lived experiences have—on the process of coming to know; on one's access to knowledge legitimated by the political system or the academy; on the uses to which one's own and others' knowing is put—varies greatly, and accounts of knowing, feminists argue, should study rather than assume it.

Furthermore, for the feminists whose work informs this discussion, the lived experience of exclusion, erasure, or exposure to abuse in science or the academy both is itself and also stands for the marginalization of women and the denial of women's worth (among other things) as knowers. To the extent that theories of knowledge, by what they include and what they exclude or overlook, explain and justify such denial, they reveal a decided ethical bias. The sources and sorts of knowing an epistemology prescribes and rewards are neither ethically nor epistemologically innocent, and quite arguably, they may be faulty.

Finally, feminists' emphasis on the centrality of lived experience in knowing draws attention to the need for

7

[margin handwritten notes:]
Rorty – postmodern point of view, contextualism, historicism; we should throw out epistemology.
★

accountability (both epistemological and moral) for theories of knowledge as well as for what counts as knowledge. Epistemologies act as "lenses" or frameworks, implicitly or explicitly shaping our sense of what can and cannot be known, what is and is not worth knowing, who can and cannot know, whether some knowledge is or is not useful, for what purposes knowledge is or should be used, and so forth. Attempts to formulate epistemological theories have often prized stability, coherence, and universalizability, even when such qualities have excluded from view the instabilities, incoherences, and particularities visible in the lived experiences of those outside the theoretical framework. This sort of exclusionary orientation may produce significant impoverishment of "knowledge projects" in all sorts of academic disciplines, including the sciences.

Even more important, however, epistemological lenses may work to keep knowers from looking at and looking into what should be seen: they may in fact foster "not-knowing." Epistemologies that make a point of being ethically accountable, like those that do not, have limits to their competence; however, they take notice of what and who is missing from the picture, and seek self- and course corrections. What needs to be done cannot be done if it is not known. Epistemologies help knowers ask, "Are we looking at this the wrong way?" and "Are we looking away from what needs to be seen?"

Feminists' ongoing critiques of the epistemological tradition have been salutary, for wider philosophical debates among theorists of knowledge as well as for discussions (for example) of teaching and curriculum reform.[12] Critique has also led to construction that conscientiously involves more, and more diverse, participants. In the process, Elizabeth Kamarck Minnich writes, feminists

> are precisely *not* in pursuit of a single epistemology, a single philosophy, a single ideology. We are trying . . . to open space for new thinking and

modes of knowing; for heretofore suppressed
voices to speak and be well heard in ways that
may express and/or call for the creation of different epistemologies.[13]

One of the keynotes of these "different epistemologies" is
that they enable knowers to see and hear the ones who have
been cast out, stepped on, marginalized; that they act as
resources for emanicipatory relationships and practices that
resist and even reverse oppression, whether it occurs at a
personal, institutional, or societal level. As feminists explore
what Lorraine Code calls the "epistemic terrain," they are
changing the way epistemology is defined and done.

Among the most fundamental insights to emerge from
both de- and reconstructive debates in feminist epistemology are these: Knowing has profound ethical implications
that show up in both liberatory and oppressive practices.
Knowing is constructed and serves purposes. Some knowing is legitimated—by a host of factors—and some is not.
Knowledge is situated: shaped, limited, and specified by the
locations of knowers, by their particular experiences, by
what works for them and what society permits to work for
them, by what matters to them and to other knowers with
more (or less) power, by what they trust and value and
whether their objects of trust and value carry any weight in
their surroundings. The relationship between what, and how,
and for what knowers know, and any or all of these factors,
is reciprocal and dialectic. Frameworks for knowing, while
they must and do aim to account for data about the world
we live in, cannot avoid the sticky ethical wicket, either.

We will return to these concerns shortly.

Getting to Luther

The questions feminist philosophers raise about epistemology are critical to the academy, the church, and the larger

society because they require careful examination of the ethical dimensions of "knowing," which are in turn crucial for our "doing." The epistemological proposal this work makes expresses and incorporates the questions and insights feminist thought in this area has generated. It also relies on a contemporary reading of Martin Luther's *theologia crucis,* or theology of the cross.[14] I have turned to Luther for several reasons.

As a Christian theologian, I feel a keen sense of accountability for my theological inheritance, shaped particularly and peculiarly by Luther. Like my theologian-contemporaries of diverse faith communities, I cannot avoid being a "next step" in the tradition; I do not wish to, either. Whether we embrace the tradition, break with it, or do some of each, it seems to me that it makes more sense to claim it than to act as if it is not ours. For better or worse— and I hope to show, in the case of the proposal this book makes, that it is for better—Luther is also part of my legacy.

More important, however, I believe that elements of this legacy, especially Luther's theology of the cross, are resources well suited to engage pressing contemporary questions whose implications, while they surely engage and affect theology, range well beyond it, too. As a feminist woman whose concerns the church's theological tradition has almost always excluded, I say this with self-awareness and conviction. It is intellectually and politically important for me to engage Christian theology generally, and Luther specifically, as a feminist. To enter into this conversation entails not only an intellectual and political, but also, frankly, an existential struggle, one I share with many other women and some men inside and outside the church. If I am able to claim, or reclaim, elements or themes—even a "sense" of what in this tradition can be of good use to those among us whom it has so often excluded—then the effort will have more than justified itself.

In terms of my particular approach to Luther, I wish to be quite clear: this book is not *about* Luther's theology of the cross.[15] Rather, it *engages* Luther's theology of the cross in a new, constructive project that also depends on thinkers and speaks to concerns that have had little previous association with Luther, his theology, or what scholars (most of them theologians) have made of his theology. This novel engagement requires that Luther's theology of the cross be presented intelligibly, fairly, and *as an invitation*—for I am convinced it is one—to those for whom neither Luther nor theology has much appeal. As a theologian who is also a feminist, I would agree heartily with Hall, who urges that even—perhaps, I would add, especially—theological work be done in "dialogue with many for whom such a theology has no meaning, but whose basic concern for humanity may in many respects be parallel and be served by it."[16] There are understandable, sometimes powerful reasons for the distances these "many" have placed or simply have left between themselves and "such a theology"; this discussion will take note of and respond to some of these reasons. But insofar as the order of business here is to offer grounds for a conversation about living a morally responsible life, grounded in what Hall calls a "basic concern for humanity," we must search out and test rigorously all available resources. I would argue that Luther's theology of the cross is among them.

From the threshold of the twenty-first century, the sixteenth-century reality to which Luther spoke is almost unimaginable. This says at least as much about the conditions of our knowing as it does about Luther in his time. There is not an aspect of our lives and the language and conceptual apparatus we use to describe them that has not been transformed materially in the intervening five centuries. While human beings surely continue to be concerned about many of the same things, it may be as difficult for us to discover

what Luther really meant, given his own time and framework, as it would have been for him to have written about
those things in terms of our context.[17]

The gap between his time and ours need not dumb-
found us. It ought, however, to render us self-conscious
about how we express Luther's truths. "When we read
Luther's writings," writes Walter Altmann, "we are always
confronted by them in a very peculiar way, which we might
share to some extent—yet never fully—with others whose
experiences, situations, convictions, and views are similar."[18]
Luther was as politically, culturally, socially, and economically engaged, as implicated in his history, setting, and
commitments, as any historical figure ever was. Awareness
of the ways in which, like Luther, we are affected by *our*
history, setting, and commitments enables us to own more
fully to what is ours about our interpretation, and to recognize the challenge to rephrase and re-present his insights,
confident that in fact he and we are wrestling with many of
the same momentous issues, both secular and religious.[19]

Luther invites frankness about these things. Almost
everything he wrote—some of which could be called "theology" only at a very long stretch—he wrote responsively,
even reactively—not systematically. Moreover, as one Luther
scholar observes,

> ...his statements are often ambiguous, sometimes
> contradictory, and occasionally unclear, [which]
> demonstrates his struggle to formulate his own
> understanding . . . . [No attempt should be made]
> to resolve internal contradictions or to erase am-
> biguities . . . [i]n other words, . . . to improve upon
> Luther himself . . . .[20]

I am convinced that, at least in principle, Luther would
appreciate the sort of project this book attempts. His conviction that there is a profoundly theological significance at

the heart of human knowing, a significance that transforms everyday life as it is lived, can help us, whether or not we share his theological framework, focus our attention on that knowing and its ethical freight and its daily consequences. That the project involves bringing unlikely partners into conversation with one another to respond—collaboratively where possible, critically where necessary—to a challenge they may be better able to meet together than either of them could alone, would, I think, appeal to Luther's sense of adventure, too.

Luther's theologizing also proceeds with utter honesty about the limits and legitimate purview of theological reflection. An unrelenting thinker and "reasoner," he seeks a certainty that eludes him except in faith. Often he seems to want to bracket, by what he does say, what cannot be said; to make sure we are clear about which things there are no grounds for claiming or knowing. It is often quite difficult to separate methodology from substance in his work.[21] Finally, there is a kind of restlessness in Luther's theology that suggests he must have struggled mightily to come to terms with some of the intellectually and spiritually difficult insights reflected there.

Resistencia . . . *and a Gift*

During the years I lived and worked in El Salvador, I spent a great deal of time shepherding around individuals or groups who came from North America or Europe to get a glimpse of the hot and dusty reality they had heard, read, protested, and prayed about from afar. Over the course of four or five days, we would spend time talking with the Mothers of the Disappeared, with representatives of a coalition of agricultural cooperatives or a federation of labor unions, with the head of Tutela Legal (the legal aid office of the Archdiocese), with personnel from the U.S. Embassy, with the nongovernmental Human Rights Commission. Military conditions and authorities permitting, we would travel to the countryside and visit a church-sponsored health project, or spend an afternoon at a refugee camp, smiling at the plentiful, barefoot, ragged, grinning children and trying to communicate with the resident mothers, grandmothers, and old men who wiped their kids' noses and distributed the tortillas and beans.

Over and over again, I witnessed this phenomenon: Those who came to visit, even for a few days, would at some point during their stay turn very quiet; they seemed to experience a kind of emotional or psychological shell shock. Sometimes the feelings came to voice—"I didn't know . . . ," "I had no idea . . . ." More often, though, I would observe these concerned and conscientious citizens stop— in the corner of a room, at a fence, on the steps of a building—silenced, looking a bit lost, trying perhaps to make some little sense of the internal welter of feeling, facts, and thought.

Sometimes, toward the end of the few days' visit, the visitors' question would come, almost painfully, to voice: "What can we do for you . . . ?" To which the Salvadorans' reply was almost invariable: "When you go back, tell them what you have seen and heard here."

This phenomenon may have made an especially lasting impression on me because I was often asked to translate: the words of those who lived the daily reality of war and poverty, for those who came to see, and the words of those who came to see, for those who taught them. Each time I did, I experienced anew the struggle—my own as well as my compatriots'—to face and relinquish the resistance to knowing: not only *about* the terrible suffering, but especially, to coming to know the actual persons—children, women, and men—who suffered. No matter how often I saw others go through this struggle, I never reached the point where I did not wrestle with it, too.

14

Before I left El Salvador to return to the United States, I made appointments to see as many of my Salvadoran colleagues as possible. I told a number of them, as we talked one last time, that I felt I needed permission, especially from them, to leave; the war was still going on, the need for economic assistance to humanitarian projects and physical "accompaniment," which had been my principal tasks, had only grown, and I could not help feeling that I was abandoning my friends. I will never forget the response of one of my closest collaborators. "My friend," she said very gently, "don't worry. You will never leave El Salvador. The only ones who leave us are the ones who forget the suffering of our people. You will never leave us."

Her words granted me the permission I had needed.

My colleague was right. Since my departure in 1986, I have lived fully—physically, emotionally, and spiritually—here in the United States. But I have carried El Salvador with me, not as a burden of guilt or nostalgia, but as a gift, a point of reference for what is important in precisely the sense my friend's words expressed.

Constructing a New Framework for Knowing

The challenge for me, as the Preface suggests, has been to find a way to translate this point of reference into a framework and a language appropriate to the place and the people I come from, to and for whom I feel accountable—not least of all because of the transformation I, as one of "my people," experienced in a far country.[22] I have not stopped struggling to face and relinquish my own resistance to knowing of the suffering of others; I doubt that I ever will stop having to struggle with this.[23] Whether I discover as I do so that I have been the cause of it (as a U.S. citizen in El Salvador, for example, I surely was), or that I benefit from it (as a white person in the United States, for example,

15

I surely do), or both, or neither, I cannot escape implication in others' suffering; I am, after all, a human being who shares the same "cruciform reality."[24] So I seek tools that may assist me in my ongoing struggle to face and relinquish my resistance to knowing what I *must* know in order to live faithfully. The agenda of this existential task must be reviewed and rewritten almost continuously.

This book describes two resources—feminist epistemologies and Luther's theology of the cross—from which an "epistemology of the cross" can be constructed. Such a framework is intended to help us as North Americans, many Christians among us, to identify both theological and epistemological criteria that will focus our attention on how and where we must look to learn what we need to know to live morally responsible lives.

" . . . [T]he cross places suffering at the heart of God's character and at the heart of meaningful, faithful human life," writes Walter Brueggemann. Precisely for this reason, he continues,

> . . . our North American dominant cultural values are massively resistant to a theology of the cross . . . . Cultural resistance to . . . suffering has as its counterpart theological resistance to the cross that issues either in . . . disregard or . . . distortion and trivialization . . . [25]

Brueggemann believes that if North Americans are to attend to the suffering that is at the heart of our lives together, and at the heart of God's life with and in us, we must seek different categories for life and understanding—categories that touch "every aspect of life, socio-economic and epistemological, as well as ethical."[26]

The construction of an epistemology of the cross is an exercise in the development of "different categories," especially those that relate our knowing to power/privilege, experience, "objectivity," and accountability. Within the dialectic of an epistemology of the cross, we find ourselves dis-illusioned, that is, enabled to see what we have resisted seeing; drawn into the reality we share with those who have been invisible to us in their suffering; and called to responsive account for what we know.

A Brief Account of What Is to Come

So far, I have argued that the relationship between knowing (or not-knowing) and doing has both instrumental and ethical significance. Generally, philosophers' analysis of and theories about knowing have focused overwhelmingly on the possibility, conditions, and justification of knowledge, paying little attention to the ethical freight both knowledge and theories about it bear. Late-twentieth-century feminist approaches both criticize inadequate and unjust approaches to knowing and suggest better and more inclusive approaches to knowledge-making. Taking account of those who have been marginalized or left out entirely, and of the ethical and epistemological consequences to them *and* to so-called bona fide knowers, requires overcoming a deep-seated and widespread resistance to knowing of others' suffering.

Luther's passionate convictions, both about humans' pretensions to know "what matters" and about the way we live (because, he believes, we do *not* know what matters), are essential ingredients of his theology of the cross. In conversation with feminist epistemologies, I will argue, the *theologia crucis* helps shape an "epistemology of the cross," a powerful resource that both describes and may facilitate a recasting of our focus and categories for knowing.

Chapter 1 provides a closer look at and analysis of feminist epistemologies, one of whose central contentions has been that both knowing and theories about it are unavoidably an ethical enterprise whose assumptions and consequences affect the way we see ourselves and our relationships with others. Traditional epistemologies have generally functioned in a way that has "totalized" on the basis of a power-privileged perspective, remaining oblivious to both their limited competence and the destructive impact of their ethical and political implications. The knowing produced by such totalizing epistemologies may be said to be "bad" in two ways: it is incomplete in the extreme, and, insofar as it keeps knowers' attention focused *away* from the extent, depth, and stubbornness of suffering in the world, it contributes to human suffering.

Feminists' critique is strengthened by constructive proposals, which underscore at least three key issues: (1) the importance of the role embodied, lived experience plays in knowing, and the complications "multiply identified" knowers introduce in sorting out this issue; (2) a reconstruction of the central epistemological notion of "objectivity" in a way that does the double duty it must do: to respond to the need for reliable knowledge about the world, and also to correspond to the ethical complexity any knowledge of the world involves; and (3) engagement with the question of what it means for knowers to be accountable both to solid epistemological standards and to one another. Feminist epistemologies insist on keeping our feet to the existential fire.

Chapter 2 brings Luther and his theology of the cross into the room. It sketches out the historical and intellectual context within which Luther's theology of the cross emerged: the early sixteenth century, a time of great upheaval in European church and society, a time of transition between one epoch and another. In this latter respect, Luther's time may be constructively, if modestly, likened to our own—perhaps with comparable spiritual, intellectual, and ethical exigencies.

This chapter then interprets the reformer's *theologia crucis* in terms of how it may be understood to function.

First, it acts as a critique of official theology but, more profoundly, of human pretension to God-ness—to know and name reality, to save themselves, to manage without God. It can also be understood as an announcement of God's loving intention toward humankind, as well as the value of embodied experience. Finally, the theology of the cross functions to equip persons to "use reality rightly," not least of all by calling things by their right names.

The players having been introduced in Chapters 1 and 2, the next chapter then proposes a conversation between them, issuing in what I will call "an epistemology of the cross." Such an epistemology acts as a framework within which to ask and respond constructively to the question, What sorts and sources of knowledge should we consider compelling as we seek to live morally responsible lives? The elements comprising this framework, especially as they relate to issues of power, experience, objectivity, and accountability, are as richly expressed in feminist terms as they are in terms "of the cross." An epistemology of the cross describes the movement from lived experience to compelling knowledge, a movement that involves seeing what is the case; comprehending one's implication in it; and coming to accept accountability to act on what is known.

Finally, for the sake of rigor and accountability, two key objections are raised. According to the first, a privileged church forfeits its claim to a theology (hence, an epistemology) of the cross insofar as it turns the cross into a blind construct, severed from the suffering experienced by real persons. When this happens, the cross and the theology it engenders work against rather than for liberation of those the church has often joined in oppressing. The response to this objection is essentially that, as Luther saw, only a privileged church *needs* a theology (and an epistemology) of the cross, which unmasks the cruciform reality this church conspires in and so often refuses to recognize. While this objection hinges here on the misappropriation of the cross by the community of people that gathers around the cross as its central symbol, it also has wide-ranging implications for persons, institutions, and nations that occupy positions that allow them to dominate and oppress others.

The second objection suggests that a theology—and therefore, an epistemology—that so depends on the bloody cross cannot avoid glorifying suffering. There is no ethically permissible defense for the multiplicity of ways in which Christian theology and Christians' practices have done just this, at the expense of millions of people over a period of almost two millenia. Many women's deep distrust of Christianity stems largely from the Church's propensity to succumb to this evil.

For his part, Luther argued that suffering ought never be sought as a "good work"; rather, he contended, it necessarily accompanies life lived as a follower of Christ. Interpreting Luther in terms of an epistemology of the cross, I contend that coming to awareness of suffering itself brings suffering, and the possibility that we may not be able to establish meaning in suffering. Acknowledgment of the reality of "the cross"—of suffering—is essential if we are to respond to it, to bear with it, and/or to overcome it. An epistemology of the cross, far from glorifying suffering, helps us see and respond to it.

The concluding chapter offers a brief illustration of how an epistemology of the cross works to illuminate the phenomenon of traumatic violence (drawing on Judith Herman's *Trauma and Recovery*) and reiterates briefly the underlying concern this book articulates: that knowing and knowers be deeply and courageously engaged in bringing forth liberating change.

Before proceeding to the substance just described, I would like to say a word or two about the style in which this book is written. Several readers of this material in its earlier incarnation as a doctoral dissertation remarked on its "autobiographical flavor" and its resemblance to an "extended essay." Although I do not take their comments, nor do I think they were meant, as criticisms, I do hear their observations as remarks on the difference between the style of this work and the style of most academic or scholarly writing.

✗ In his *God of the Oppressed*, James H. Cone observes that

> [t]heologians do not normally reveal the true source of their theological reflections. . . . More often than not, it is a theologian's *personal* history . . . that serves as the most important factor in shaping the methodology and content of his or her theological perspective. . . . [T]heologians ought to be a little more honest. . . .[27]

For me, scholarship and the thinking, knowing, and writing it entails have both an intensely personal and a fundamentally provisional character. I believe this is true for most feminist scholars—and for Luther, too. What this means is woven into and worked out through the course of these pages and the arguments they hold. I would not have written about any of this if it did not matter a great deal to me and to those I care about most passionately. What is autobiographical about this book, then, is reflected as much in the theological and ethical ideas I dispute and propose as it is in the stories, events, and feelings I name as my own. I would hope that the convictions and commitments I reveal here strengthen, not diminish, the value and cogency of the intellectual project.

Feminist Epistemologies: Critiques and Concerns

Feminists' thinking about epistemology, like feminists' thinking about almost everything else, has become much more nuanced, variegated—and interesting—over the course of several decades. As Sandra Harding observes,

> Feminist analyses . . . are not monolithic. There is no single set of claims beyond a few generalities that could be called "feminism" . . . . [F]eminism is itself a contested zone not only within feminism but also between feminism and its critics.[1]

Thanks to wake-up calls issued by women of color, lesbian women, Third World women, and women with disabilities, among others, against their automatic and inappropriate inclusion in categories designed by and about relatively privileged, white, heterosexual, Euro-American women, feminist thought and practice have moved toward greater recognition of the astonishing variety of women and women's experiences.[2] Few feminists missed the irony of the fact that second-wave feminist thinkers who had protested the inclusion and consequent effective erasure of women in the male-defined generic category "man" themselves invited a not altogether dissimilar course-correcting admonition.[3] In fact, the intrafeminist stir generated by questions of difference, diversity, identity, and so forth, has resulted in a mix of far richer, more nuanced, and more useful contemporary conversations about a variety of issues that affect women's lives. The following discussion seeks to keep in mind some of the lessons taught and learned at the feminist roundtable.

As the introduction pointed out, feminist thinkers who have made epistemology their business have moved it out of the philosophical seminar room and into the larger, public stage of society and culture where the politics and ethics that attach to knowing, knowers, and knowledge neither can nor should be avoided. Feminist epistemologies are especially remarkable in that they do not argue whether knowledge is possible or not, that is, they do not engage the traditional epistemological issues. Instead, they question the terms of the enterprise itself, an approach that would not be possible without the critical perspective they commend to all who deal in epistemological questions, a perspective variously articulated but fervently shared by feminists of all descriptions.

The basis on which they describe and question the terms of traditional epistemology is a twofold inadequacy: scientific and moral, or ethical. While these two types of inadequacy can be distinguished, feminists say, they cannot be separated. Ultimately—and even in the shorter run—the kind of science we do and the kind of moral deliberation we engage in depend on epistemological assumptions and categories, even on which questions we ask about knowing and which ones we do not ask; it also affects the way we see ourselves and the sort of relationships we have with others. Bodies of knowledge and practice (like science) affect self-identity and relationships by shaping them, explaining them, justifying them, institutionalizing them, and perpetuating them.

Those who have a hand in forming and those who chiefly benefit from what Elizabeth Kamarck Minnich calls the "dominant meaning system"[4] would seem to have least incentive to entertain countervailing views. They have the luxury of not noticing, perhaps because they do not need to notice, the destructive consequences their epistemological framework brings with it. In addition, feminists argue, the powerfully positioned have the least developed capacity to assume, even intellectually, a position that is critical of—"over against"—their own scientific (and ethical) projects. Such a critical disposition is key to producing and advancing science; the rub is that the advances realized because of such critical "over-against-ness" always also strengthen the possibility of undermining dominance based on the power to limit voices of critique or dissent.

This chapter functions to describe my own commitment to a feminist approach to questions of knowing and my interest in appropriating this approach vis-à-vis epistemology and, further along, the theological-ethical proposal toward which this project aims. It also intends to elucidate this approach in a way that justifies such a commitment. Key feminist treatments of epistemological questions, particularly those of Sandra Harding, Donna Haraway, Lorraine Code, and Elizabeth Kamarck Minnich, will act as points of reference.

These and other feminist thinkers have engaged with epistemology in two principal ways, which will organize the discussion that follows. First, they have brought a profound critique to bear on the approach to epistemology taken by those who represent the post-Enlightenment Western philosophical tradition. From several angles, this critique, focused primarily on how science is done, has targeted "totalizing theories" that have tended to exclude or leave out those considered unreliable or unworthy "knowers," especially women. Inattention to the ethical and political freight borne by such theories and by the knowing they sanction and frame is another key complaint feminist thinkers raise in relation to traditional epistemology.

Feminist writers have also generated a good deal of constructive work. Some of this work responds to questions such as What is or ought feminist epistemology be? Can there be such a thing? How might feminist epistemologies contribute to a larger liberatory project? Few feminists insist on a single approach to "feminist epistemology"; increasingly, contributors to the conversation focus on clarifying those elements and themes they believe essential to a liberatory epistemology. Among these are the roles experience plays in knowing, especially in view of multiply identified knowers, the difficulties of retaining some useful, nontotalizing understanding of "objectivity"; and what it means for knowers to be accountable to one another and to a shared future.

The following discussion will begin with the feminist critique of traditional epistemology and its impact and an assessment of the constructive tasks facing feminist epistemologists. It will then describe and comment on how experience, objectivity, and accountability figure in feminist approaches to knowers, knowing, and knowledge.

I. *Traditional Epistemology Characterized*

Epistemology "made by professional philosophers of the mainstream," Lorraine Code contends, "is one of the more arcane and esoteric artifacts of men[,] . . . in the main, of white men."[6] Historically, and most broadly, it has dealt mainly with the issues of whether knowledge is possible[7] and if it is, what conditions are necessary and sufficient to define and discuss it; and what sort of relationship exists between knowledge and reality. These tasks have been predicated on a vision, born in the Enlightenment, according to which the human mind could reflect perfectly an existing world "out there" that is ready and able to be reflected. That is, there *is* something really there, and it is possible for human observers to position themselves to *see* what is really there—nature and social life—as they really are. Both the questions raised and the resolutions philosophers have reached generally have been and are phrased in terms of "all men," not just philosophers. To claim this sort of universality reflects, at its best, the broad significance philosophers believe these matters have, as well as the possibility that their resolution will have the same long reach; at its worst, the blanket "all men" makes differences disappear and suffocates critical inquiry that might improve the questions and notice the impact of their resolutions.

Western science, seeking to underwrite knowledge about what is "really there," wants to tell "one true story"—somewhat like a multi-million-piece jigsaw puzzle whose pieces, however numerous, still all fit together—rather than live with the ambiguity that may well exist and might persist if science confined itself to trying to tell less false stories. In pursuit and defense of "one true story," stable and coherent theories and categories, and what Sandra Harding, recalling Descartes' language, describes as a "powerful transcendental Archimedean standpoint,"[8] have great value, even when the former may not account for actual instabilities and incoherences, and the latter may not exist in real life.

The central assumptions underlying traditional epistemology, which are most clearly expressed in modern science, are taken to be value-free, neutral, and universally applicable. Those who make either science or knowledge rarely acknowledge the effects that the wider cultural, political, or social contexts may have on their activities, a state of things attributable in large measure to the high status of scientific knowledge. The alleged value-free character of scientific knowledge, according to which "values" and "facts" can be (and usually are) strictly separated, confers on those who pursue it a freedom from preoccupation with how the knowledge that "facts" comprise will be used.[9] "The separation . . . between facts and values," Lorraine Code writes,

> supports the conclusion that facts are "just facts" and worth pursuing for their own sake. Questions about the social and/or moral consequences of discovery can, consequently, be designated as separate matters with which . . . knowledge seekers . . . need not . . . concern themselves.[10]

Little account is taken of the interpretive nature of scientific descriptions—that they are, as Donna Haraway observes, "produced, not just innocently available."[11]

The knower in mainstream epistemology is, Code writes, "a featureless abstraction," not a person with individual capacities, location, interests, and so forth, each and all of which might affect—though not necessarily distort—his or her observations.[12] The knower/subject and the known/object occupy different causal planes; neither their relationship nor the knowledge the knower/subject generates is negotiated or reciprocal. Instead, according to this mainstream epistemological model, the knower/subject has a kind of nonsymmetrical power over the known/object, whether that is a chemical reaction, a social system, or another person. The subordination of the known/object creates an "other," whose contributions to knowledge become part of the knower's "material." Such relationships of super- and subordination underwrite the illusion of epistemological control and relieve the anxiety epistemological ambiguity can produce.

In suggesting a typology of four major errors that characterize not only *what* but also *how* (we think) we know, Minnich has summarized some of the key practical consequences of epistemology-as-usual. "The dominant culture," she writes, as complex and contradictory and many-voiced as it is, is built on *faulty generalizations* (taking a particular "kind" of people, works, acts to be generic, representative, inclusive, normative for all), and *circular reasoning* (by which "kinds" are selected as generic, et al); historically, abstractions are derived from them; and then those abstractions are used to justify the continuing centrality and normativity of the kinds from which they were abstracted in the first place, which lead to *mystified concepts*, such as a notion of excellence that conflates it with exclusivity (that hide and thereby perpetuate those errors) and thence to *partial knowledge* that claims generality.[13]

"Faulty generalization" both emanates from and helps to create the "one true story" approach to epistemology. What belongs to the critically most *real* category, for example, comes to define both what is within *and* what is outside the chief category; what is within is valued, while what is outside is devalued, considered less important, deviant, or helpful only insofar as it describes the truly valued.[14] As Minnich points out, generalizations are not necessarily faulty; they are, however, when they function to exclude on the basis of hierarchy and power.

"Circular reasoning" proves the truth of an assertion by defining as irrelevant whatever might disprove it on the basis that anything that might disprove it is irrelevant. If it is true, for example, that scientific knowledge is value-free or (even) transcendent, then any claim that knowledge reflects the interests or values of those who produce it, or any claim that knowledge is "situated," is ruled out by virtue of the prior assertion—which is itself a close relative of "faulty generalization."

Excellence, judgment, equality, intelligence, woman, sex, man, and gender exemplify what Minnich calls "mystified

29

concepts." These and others, because of both how they have been mystified and how they mystify, are particularly persistent because what they mean, how they are used, and what effect their use has, are so seldom scrutinized. Their invocation often stops critical thinking, conversation, and dissent from prevailing but largely implicit understandings of what these concepts actually entail. Sheila Briggs' observations about the evident commensurability between white, male, middle-class identity and the definition of equality illustrate what Minnich means by a mystified concept, and how the mystification of one (equality) is implicated in the mystification of another (human nature):

> Those who do not share this particular identity have access to equal treatment only when their identity is "overlooked." Hence, to be black, or hispanic, or female, or on welfare becomes detrimental to one's claim to equality, unless one appeals to a more "fundamental" human nature. It then becomes "unfair" to treat such persons with regard to their sex, race, or class, because this would prejudice their rights. And it becomes "unfair" to treat white middle-class males with regard to their sex, race or class, because this would grant them undue privilege.[15]

In their ambiguity and opacity, mystified concepts can be fashioned easily into platitudes and pieties, invoked without fear of challenge and therefore capable of wielding great power in service of an exclusionary status quo.[16]

By "partial knowledge," Minnich means knowledge, established by the dominant tradition, that is partial in two senses: "It makes the part the whole, and that whole is partial to the interests of those thus enshrined at the defining, controlling center."[17] This error, which overlaps with "faulty generalization," focuses particular attention on the role of power in establishing what will be ac*knowledge*d as true, important, real. Knowledge is what is known by those whose knowing is recognized as "knowledge"; rules, boundaries, definitions, criteria regulate the process of coming to know and of recognizing that knowing. Some regulation occurs through professions, disciplines, and language; much of it is implicit, but not arbitrary, at least not from the viewpoint of those who hold power. Even to disagree with the regulation of knowledge is to recognize the rules of the debate. Those who refuse to enter into the debate according to conventional rules are shut out, and those who violate them are thought dangerous to good order: epistemologically, academically, even politically.

To question the ethical or scientific adequacy—or the usefulness—of traditional epistemology is, in traditional epistemological terms, heretical.

2 · *The Impact of Epistemology-As-Usual*

Embedded epistemological assumptions—both "positive" ones having to do with who qualifies as a knower, the separation of facts and values, the relation between knower and known, and so forth, and "negative" ones that obviate the need to ask *who* knows and what knowing might be *for*, for example—have profound implications in many quarters. Code observes, for example, that

> institutionalized disciplines that produce knowledge about women, and position women in societies according to the knowledge they produce, are informed by versions of and variations on the methods and objectives that received epistemologies authorize . . . .[18]

Key feminist critics of "received epistemologies" have focused on science and philosophy as knowledge-producing

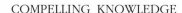

and women-positioning disciplines; their analyses have pride of place in what follows. It is important to note that the high regard accorded "scientific" knowledge, as well as the tenacity of "faulty [philosophical] generalizations" carry the epistemological assumptions that underlie them into all sorts of nonscientific, nonphilosophical conversations about knowing and knowers. It is also worth pointing out that explicit feminist critiques of traditional epistemology are emerging in other disciplines, including bioethics and theology.[19]

The language of these disciplines as they have been written and taught in the academy and in the professions has traditionally, consistently communicated the inferiority of women in a host of ways. Specifically, it has assumed that they are "incapable of having knowledge of the best and most rational kind."[20] "Woman the knower" has been understood to be a contradiction in terms; as Harding points out, convention has held that to be "scientific" has meant "to be dispassionate, disinterested, impartial, concerned with abstract principles and rules," while to be a woman has meant "to be emotional, interested in and partial to the welfare of family and friends, concerned with concrete practices and contextual relations."[21] Such assumptions provide the basis on which to exclude women from teaching, research, policy-making, and other positions that by "convention" "require" qualities women are not thought to have—on the grounds of the same conventional epistemological assumptions.

Without regard to gender, learners absorb lessons that define knowing, knowledge, and knowers in terms that grant privilege to some and exclude other classes of knowing, knowledge, and knowers. Donna Haraway observes, "If our experience is of domination, we will theorize our lives according to principles of dominance."[22] If we have learned to make sense of our experience—to "know" it—in terms that explain, rationalize, and implicitly or explicitly defend relations of such domination as "natural" or at least "given," then we will be less likely to question our places, whether

32

we are on the short or the long end of the stick. Without the categories to notice and name the emperor's nakedness, we are likely to applaud his procession—and to join in silencing the voice of an impertinent child. "Insofar as we speak and think and act in ways that make sense to other people within the dominant meaning system," Minnich writes, "we cannot avoid participating . . . in precisely that which we wish to change."[23]

To name the significant dimensions of my own location may be a partial antidote to such participation. Explicitly, it entails acknowledging my limitations: not so much what they are, since I do not know exactly what they are, but rather that I have them. To acknowledge that I have them, in turn, is to acknowledge that there is much I do not know, that I need to hear from other sources, to hear other voices. It means, too, that I have a contribution to make, and that it is a particular contribution, not a universal declaration, to the conversation. It also means that I do want to be part of a conversation.

Implicitly, naming my own coordinates identifies me in relation to others like me, pulls at me to identify myself in relation to those who are like me and in some way to articulate the accountability I have to whom I have it. Doing so also distinguishes me from those who do not share significantly in my location, and in some way makes it incumbent on me to account for myself to them.

Even so, as Minnich reminds us, the temptation to lose consciousness and a restless, critical edginess over against "the dominant meaning system" is virtually irresistible—probably for everyone, but perhaps especially for women who enjoy relatively more privilege within that system. Here, the panoply of different women's voices mentioned at the beginning of this chapter may serve to strengthen resistance. The words Maria Lugones addresses to white women theorists might almost as easily have been addressed (by Lugones or by her addressees) to men of privilege:

> Plurality speaks to you of a world . . . that you
> inhabit unwillingly[,] . . . a world inhabited by be-
> ings who cannot be understood given your ordi-
> nary notions of responsibility, intentionality, . . .
> precisely because those notions presuppose that
> each person is one and each person . . . can effec-
> tively inform her actions . . . all by herself. All other
> ways of being are outside value . . . .[24]

Even for women who share with one another a deep commitment to transforming a reality in which women are sub-
ordinated, "multiple identities"—some relatively privileged,
some marginalized—surely present substantial challenges both
intra- and interpersonally. Epistemology-as-usual is no re-
specter of persons; for feminists, however, its internalized
effects may seem doubly pernicious.

There is another, related issue. Feminist thinkers have
launched their critiques of epistemology-as-usual from the
solid if varied terrain of women's life experiences; their
analyses have gathered intellectual steam and moral passion
because of their attention to its impact on women's lives.
From the start, they observed a long Western philosophical
and theological history associating women with nature ("objectivity" expressed the control the Man of Reason—Descartes
was an exemplar—sought, through "knowing," to exert over
nature; women were "by nature" incapable of realizing this
epistemological ideal).[25] More recently, however, feminists
have begun to draw together the threads of what are often
referred to as "interlocking" oppressions—those that are
based not only on gender but also, for example, on class,
race, and sexual orientation. While these different forms of
oppression have different histories and contemporary dynamics, epistemology-as-usual has tended to deny access to
marginalized knowers and refused to recognize as "real"
knowledge produced by groups who suffer these forms of
oppression. Many feminists have sought to make common

epistemological cause with, as well as deepen their informed respect for, those for whom the struggle against domination has a different starting point.

3. *Assessing the Tasks of Feminist Epistemologies*

Those who expect theories of knowledge, the stock in trade of traditional epistemological inquiry, to deal with the experiences of knowing that ordinary knowers have on a daily basis or with the place, value, or dilemmas of knowing in people's lives, or to help shape ways of describing how the world is that will help transform it toward something better, are not likely to get much help from epistemology-as-usual. "As the map [of the epistemic terrain] is currently drawn," Code writes,

> there is no place for analyses of the availability of knowledge, of knowledge-acquisition processes, or—above all—of the political considerations that are implicated in knowing anything more interesting than the fact that the cup is on the table, now.[26]

Knowers who have the privilege to define the proper quarter of epistemology in terms of the possibility of knowledge of cups on tables, now, are likely to be those who have had the luxury to choose to confine their reflections to such types of knowledge. Power and politics, as has been suggested, play important roles in shaping and pursuing epistemological agendas; and the outcomes of these agendas, whatever their philosophical value, must also be read ethically.

The questions mainstream epistemology has asked may have narrowed its scope too much. In suggesting a host of additional questions, feminist theorists of knowledge break open the field of inquiry. "Who can be subjects, agents, of socially legitimate knowledge?" Harding asks.

35

What kinds of things can be known? . . . Can . . .
socially situated truths count as knowledge? . . .
What is the nature of objectivity? Does it require
point-of-viewlessness? . . . What should be the
purposes of the pursuit of knowledge? Can there
be "disinterested knowledge" in a society that is
deeply stratified by gender, race, and class?[27]

Most of these questions and the responses to them have
been implicit in the program of conventional epistemology.
Now, however, they have been raised explicitly: from a
critical stance, from the lives of those whose experiences
have not fit the "regularities" social scientists have sought to
explain using conventional epistemological assumptions. As
a result, more often than not " . . . a 'line of fault' opens up
between [women's] experiences of their lives and the dominant conceptual schemes."[28]

A preliminary assessment of the tasks feminist epistemologies face surely reveals the need to continue to
deconstruct epistemology-as-usual and the science theories
and practices that depend on it insofar as these act to erase,
exploit, or marginalize persons, particularly women. Minnich
maintains that this has been and remains the task of feminist
scholars and activists "not because the task *could* not be
taken on by non-feminists, but because it *has* not been . . . ."[29]
Others would argue, instead, that women and/or other disenfranchised people are singularly positioned to engage it.

Furthermore, epistemological proposals, even as they
seek to satisfy our shared human need for reliable, useful
knowledge, must also be held ethically accountable. These
two requirements are inextricably linked, as the foregoing
feminist critiques of traditional epistemological approaches
make clear. The criteria an epistemology offers for determining who can be a knower; what tests beliefs must pass
in order to be legitimated as knowledge; and what kinds of
things can be known, signal implicit and explicit ethical

(and political) agendas. Cloaked in the mystified concepts and faulty generalizations of which Minnich writes, these agendas are rarely exposed and corrected as needed. Feminist thinkers argue that such agendas, whatever their content, should be held accountable; the alternatives they propose invite ethical as well as "scientific" scrutiny.

The accountability feminists refer to here requires that the injustices done with the help of traditional theories of knowledge be revealed in all their depth and breadth. But it also requires that new epistemologies be developed that generate what Code calls "emanicipatory effects."[30] What we do bears intimate relation with what we know—and vice versa—in both science and everyday life; we must pay close attention to the ways we can and do shape that relation, especially when we qualify or disqualify certain knowers and kinds of knowing.

In the critical and constructive work feminists are doing, several key themes emerge repeatedly; reflection about these themes is contributing substantially to the development of new epistemologies. In what follows I will discuss three of them: experience, objectivity, and accountability. As will become clear, they can be treated as discrete themes only if their mutual implication is heard as a continuous background harmony.

Ƴ. Experience

The notion of "lived experience" counts heavily in feminist thought. Feminists use the modifier *lived* to secure the value of information and insights (knowledge) gained from having lived, from having "been there," where what the knowing is about is occurring. "Lived experience" authorizes the knowing associated with it in a way that "experience" as an abstract, universalized epistemological concept does not. The frank critique feminists imply in distinguishing "lived experience" from "experience" as a philosophical concept responds to the fact that traditional epistemological theories and the systems of knowledge they support have more often than not ignored, underrated, or excluded the knowing that issued from the "lived experience" of women.

"Lived experience" suggests a legitimate claim to knowing at least some kinds of things and people. It also makes clear that the "thing or two" one may have learned by virtue of having "lived" counts as knowledge. To assign positive epistemological value to lived experience means to recognize explicitly the embodiment of knowing: not so much its concreteness but its incarnate character. As Beverly Wildung Harrison observes, "all our knowledge, including our moral knowledge, is body-mediated."[31] This dimension may not be all there is to all knowing, but conventional epistemologies usually ignore its significance altogether. In order to be persuasive or plausible, a theory of knowing must take account of lived experience.

For many women and men, the notion of "lived contradiction" is likely to accompany epistemological respect for lived experience. As feminism's second wave gathered momentum in the 1970s, lived contradictions were often described as "click!" experiences: accepted "wisdom"—what "everyone" knew to be true, say, about women—was experienced (with an accompanying Aha-like "click!") as baloney by women themselves. Minnich's "mystified concepts" are replete with such contradictions; discovered in the course of the activities of daily living and conversation, they spark recognition and then critique. "Universal" principles like equal rights are not usually color- or gender- or class-blind; and what "most people" consider "normal" relationships or behaviors neither commends the "normal" nor condemns the "non-normal." Theories of knowledge invite scrutiny from those who have experienced lived contradictions.

But what counts as "experience"? Feminists rightly criticized traditional theories of knowledge for their failure to include the epistemological fruits of "women's experience"; what these critics discovered, however, was that it is as difficult to identify and collect all the building blocks of that notion as it is to find something essential at its core. Modifying the original expression from "women's experience" to "women's experience*s*" lessens the danger of lumping "women" together and implying that their experiences have something fundamental in common, but it does not fully resolve the uneasiness. The wider the conceptual net is cast in an effort to round up evidence, the more specificity is lost—and with it, the consciousness and contributions of those specific lives that did not fit the mold of (androcentric) generality in the first place.

"'Women's experience' does not pre-exist as a kind of prior resource, ready simply to be appropriated . . . ," Donna Haraway observes, any more than *any* "sort" of experience precedes its articulation by means of "particular social occasions, the discourses, and other practices." As experience becomes articulated in itself, she argues, it also becomes articulable with other experiences, which in turn enables "the construction of an account of *collective* experience."[32] The collective experience thus accounted for—say, "women's experience"—is characterized by contradictions, connections, differences, distinctions, tensions, and affinities (rather than identities), none of which disappears simply because all have been gathered under the same rubric. It continues to be the "nature" of "women's experience" that it is, Haraway would say, "structured within multiple and often inharmonious agendas."[33]

It is no small accomplishment to recognize the heterogeneity of "agendas" that comprise "women's experience." Intellectually and, particularly, epistemologically, such recognition cohabits with resistance to totalizing assumptions about who may know and what knowledge is valued. Ethically, it depends on willingness to be held accountable *to* others *for* one's own agenda/s. And, one might add, politically, it involves renouncing the exercise of power as domination, wherever that might be an option.

The multiple-agendas plot continues to thicken if the focus shifts from the collectivity of women to the individual woman, who experiences her life in what Sheila Briggs calls "a multiplicity of identities."[34] According to Briggs, one person's identities of race, class, gender, and sexual orientation (to name only some of the weightiest variables used to distinguish humans from one another) may place him or her on both sides of what is culturally dominant. Each of these identities has its own history, in society's as well as in the individual's life, and its own peculiar meanings—again, societally and personally. Some identities may confer privilege on, others stigmatize, the same individual; society frequently metes out rewards and punishments for certain identities only to those who actually claim, or disclaim, them. As Briggs says, "To live with differently stigmatized identities, or with a combination of stigmatized and privileged identities, makes it hard sometimes to find one's face in the mirror."[35] Identity is no more a "prior resource" than experience is; identity, too, becomes articulated and articulable—even within each person. Multiple identities do not undergo homogenization into a smooth and easily managed blend; instead, they jostle, poke, disturb, and even exclude one another as often as they enrich, complement, and build each other up: all of this, within one person!

Perhaps it is a reflection of what Briggs calls the "fragmentation"[36] of which the social world, like our identities, partakes—and what Haraway calls "the always already fallen apart structure of the world"[37]—that the most difficult struggles, inter- and intrapersonally, occur because perceived and real privileges and stigmas are associated with our multiple agendas and identities. Power and conflict characterize these struggles; feminists would say that accountability must, too.

There is no innocent, no nonresponsible, no "outside" position from which to engage in these struggles. To argue, as feminist epistemological critiques do, that women have been and continue to be marginalized in and by theories of knowledge that dominate the history of Western philosophy, and that this marginalization has had and continues to have terrible human costs, which women pay disproportionately, is not to let women off the hook. As Code points out, "The [feminist epistemological] project demands an ongoing consciousness of the fact that an inquirer is implicated in every inquiry and is as culturally and historically constituted as any of her allies, collaborators, or subjects of study."[38] Her observation applies as much to the informal setting of everyday life as to formal academic research and scholarship.

The concern that women's status as bona fide knowers be recognized is the ubiquitous partner of the critique that they have not been so recognized. And the constructive work feminist thinkers continue to do in epistemology aims precisely at making contributions to the larger project that, in taking women's exclusion seriously, help ensure broader participation in that project. This means, among other things, that the complicated, delicate questions of whether and how women participate in oppressive as well as in liberatory agendas have to be dealt with forthrightly. This was a particularly discomfiting matter for feminist theologian Sharon D. Welch, whose self-awareness about her "double identity" generated great resonance in me when I first read her *Communities of Resistance and Solidarity*, perhaps because it seemed I had much in common with her, including having had a quite significant experience in war-torn Central America. She wrote:

> For me, to be a Christian is to become aware of the degree to which I am a participant in structures of oppression, structures of race, class, and

national identity. As a woman, I am oppressed by the structures of patriarchy. Yet as white, I benefit from the oppression of people of other races. As a person whose economic level is middle-class, I am both victim and victimizer of others. As an American, I live within a nation whose policies are economically, politically, and environmentally disastrous for far too many of the world's peoples.[39]

Welch called her book "an attempt to respond to [her] 'double identity'"; for me it was not coincidental that her book dealt theologically with epistemological themes, including what counts as knowledge, whose knowledge is privileged, what the relation is between experience and knowledge, and so forth. Significantly, her recognition of a double identity—or perhaps more precisely, a "set" of conflictive identities—led not to moral paralysis but to acceptance of the challenge it represented, and to engagement.

Feminist writers have tended to grant favored epistemological status to what Haraway calls "the vantage points of the subjugated." Her justification of this favor is worth quoting at some length:

The standpoints of the subjugated . . . are preferred because in principle they are least likely to allow denial of the critical and interpretative core of all knowledge. They are savvy to modes of denial through repression, forgetting, and disappearing acts—ways of being nowhere while claiming to see comprehensively. The subjugated have a decent chance to be on to the god-trick . . . . [Their] standpoints are preferred because they seem to promise more adequate, sustained, objective, transforming accounts of the world.[40]

Women's experience of subjugation as knowers sparks insights illuminating a wider conversation about knowing that invites participation from both men and women. As Harding points out, however, it is not women's experiences in themselves that ground knowledge reliably. Rather, the process of recognizing how the experience of domination is put together and maintained (at the expense of some and for the benefit of others), and of struggling against this domination, may provide a solid epistemological base.[41]

At the same time, no position, not even subjugation, intrinsically exempts the one who occupies it from critical reflection, deconstruction, and reconstruction. These essential epistemological activities thrive on the dissonances that exist within collectivities of knowers, and within individual knowers, when "'who we are' is in at least two places at once: outside and within, margin and center."[42] Along these lines, bell hooks describes one of the formidable gifts of the "outsider-within" standpoint that her mother taught her, namely, the "power to be able to separate useful knowledge that I might get from the dominating group from participation in ways of knowing that would lead to estrangement, alienation, and worse—assimilation and cooptation."[43] Those in relatively more privileged positions (by virtue of the preponderance of "advantage" among their multiple identities) have much to learn from "outsiders within"; they may learn something about the perspective from the margins, but they may also learn to see themselves with greater clarity. Code is persuaded of the possibility of realizing an equitable "conversational format" in which "no participant need deny the unique contribution that her interim privilege or lack thereof enables her to make."[44]

Experience, then, counts heavily in feminist epistemological proposals. But experience is understood as "lived," a generator of consciousness-awakening contradictions, and a shaper of the particularity of persons (rather than an homogenizer). Each one's experiences play a part in the creation of what turn out to be multiple identities, which in turn have a hand in organizing each one's experiences. The negotiation of what we have in common because of our experiences is as much a challenge to our sense of responsibility as is the recognition of our differences.[45]

5. Objectivity

Objectivity is, as Code says, one of the key "regulative principles"[46] governing any serious discussion of epistemology, especially as it takes up the issues of what—about the knower, the method of coming to know, and (sometimes) the object of knowledge—legitimates real "knowledge" even as it denies that status to beliefs and mere opinions. Rigorous scientific standards ensure objectivity. Objectivity ensures trustworthiness, in knowledge-seeking as well as in adjudicating matters of "justice." Objectivity denotes levelheadedness, dispassion, clarity of perception, the setting aside of partisan interests. Objectivity is generally held in high regard.

Feminist projects in epistemology take the matter of objectivity very seriously. While much of what feminists have to say about it is quite critical—as we shall briefly review—the quality of their criticism suggests that they are not as interested in dispensing with objectivity as they are in "separat[ing it] from its shameful and damaging history"[47] and reclaiming for it a constructive rather than an exclusive and, frankly, unrealistic epistemological function.[48]

In fact it may make more sense to ask how objectivity *functions* than to ask what it is. Admittedly, to begin with the question of function reveals some skepticism about objectivity's reputation as the last word in justifying our acceptance of something as "true." (Objectivity may be another of those "mystified concepts" Minnich has sensitized us to.) Asking how it functions, however, probably will give us a better angle on its several dimensions. It will also draw us into the question of whether we can do without objectivity; relativism hovers, which makes everyone (perhaps especially feminists) nervous.[49] In the end feminist conversation about objectivity turns constructive, offering some novel angles of its own.

Objectivity's good name seems to be built on the conviction, too simply stated here, that reality is "out there" and that its components can be "objectified"—in some crucial sense, held apart from and over against those who observe—and known. "Objectivity" in this sense is better renamed "objectivism." As discussed earlier in this chapter, the respective roles objects and subjects play in knowing are distinct and nonreciprocal: objects are the "know-ees" and subjects, the "know-ers." Assuming the rules of the game are strictly adhered to, objectivity-as-objectivism becomes a way of indicating the correspondence between reality and our epistemological grip on it.[50]

According to this view, value-free perspectives exist and must be maintained. The objectivist view is, in a curious way, the view from nowhere[51]; because reality *is* in principle accessible to "objective" observers, it does not matter precisely where they are: they could be anywhere and the view would still be the same, if the observers *are* in fact "objective." (There is a certain circularity about the reasoning.) Social causes do not—cannot—bear serious epistemological weight, except as an interesting gloss on the harder evidence that establishes the "objective" truth about something. Knowledge production must (implying it *can*) be protected from politics. When "objective" knowledge is challenged, "ideology" or "politics" is sure to be accused of playing a subversive role.

One of the most trenchant criticisms of this sort of objectivity-as-objectivism comes from Harding, who writes,

[W]e have no conception of objectivity that enables us to distinguish the scientifically "best descriptions and explanations" from those that fit most closely (intentionally or not) with the assumptions that elites in the West do not want critically examined.[52]

Unless there is a conception of objectivity, or an alternative to it, that makes room for critical treatment of dominant assumptions, scientific or other, "best descriptions and explanations" will be a category empty of epistemological value.

But what happens if we do give up on objectivity? If an insistence on objectivity is predicated on the conviction that there is a knowable, "one-true-story" sort of reality, then its counterpart, relativism, may be said to rest on the conviction (or, in some, incite the fear) that there is no such thing. At its best, relativism in epistemology means that "there is no universal, unchanging framework or scheme for rational adjudication among competing knowledge claims."[53] At its worst, relativism assigns primary epistemological value to the productions of personal subjectivity, the expressions of an individual's spontaneous consciousness. In any case, all knowledge is constructed and socially located. If this is true, what possibility exists for reliable, solid knowledge? Relativism may be, as Haraway suggests, "the perfect mirror twin of totalization in the ideologies of objectivity; both . . . [promise] vision from everywhere and nowhere equally and fully."[54]

Like objectivity-as-objectivism, however, relativism may be better understood in terms of its function. Harding observes that relativism as an epistemological issue, and value, emerged in Europe in the nineteenth century: "[It] was a safe stance for Europeans to choose; the reciprocity of respect it appeared to support had little chance of having to be enacted."[55] In any case, it may be that relativism becomes a problematic (rather than a helpful) construct when the views of those who dominate are being challenged.

When established relations of power (and the theories of knowledge that sanction them) are threatened, the fallout can make it seem as if the world—or at least the one true story about it—is coming to an end. "Relativism" becomes the intellectual equivalent of the plague.

What makes the tension between "objectivity" and "relativism" interesting in the context of the present discussion is that feminist epistemologists are no more eager than anyone else to dispense with either one. Haraway describes the parameters of the problem:

> . . . "[O]ur" problem is how to have *simultaneously* an account of radical historical contingency for all knowledge claims and knowing subjects . . . *and* a no-nonsense commitment to faithful accounts of a "real" world, one that can be partially shared and friendly to earth-wide projects of finite freedom, adequate material abundance, modest meaning in suffering, and limited happiness.[56]

It is perhaps not surprising that, even as she describes the problem, Haraway affirms what a review of feminist epistemological work suggests: "In traditional philosophical categories, the issue is ethics and politics perhaps more than epistemology."[57] Her clarification is helpful, especially for those who are skeptical (to say the least) about whether what Haraway and others are doing really is epistemology. However, the point of this new work is precisely that it adapts and augments the epistemological vocabulary to enable talk about knowing to correspond to what makes the notion of "objectivity" so difficult to specify in the midst of daily living. Here, feminists argue, to neglect—among other matters— how power and privilege help define legitimate knowers and knowledge, and how and whom privilege-legitimated knowing serves, is to free epistemology from any accountability. Drifting untethered over the political and moral landscape, it remains an abstraction, an intellectual hot-air balloon, with no discernible connection with the embodied reality of actual people's lives.

Coming up with a usable understanding of objectivity that acknowledges the constructedness of both knowledge and epistemology's terms of reference, on the one hand, and yet offers rigor and reliability, on the other, involves a degree of intellectual imaginativeness not usually associated with the term. Harding believes that in the wider conversation about objectivity, feminists must—remarkably—insist on tougher standards. What she calls "strong objectivity" requires critical identification and evaluation of the *causes* of human beliefs—even, or maybe especially, those powerful background beliefs that have long passed for "objective truths." " . . . [E]ven if the ideal of identifying all the causes of human beliefs is rarely if ever achievable," Harding asks, "why not hold it as a desirable standard?"[58] Strong objectivity may be seen to extend the notion of scientific research to include systematic examination of mystified concepts and faulty generalizations.

How can this be accomplished? We must "start thought . . . from multiple lives that are in many ways in conflict with one another and each of which has its own multiple and contradictory commitments."[59] Among these "multiple lives" and "multiple and contradictory commitments" we are perhaps best advised to start from the less favored positions—those whose peculiar partiality[60] has a good chance of alerting us to the distortions we cannot see when we are comfortably ensconced, or entrenched, in them. Haraway's observation about what she calls the "knowing self" suggests what makes it possible for us to enter into this process:

> [It] is partial in all its guises, never finished, whole, simply there and original; it is always constructed and stitched together imperfectly, and *therefore*

able to join with another, to see together without claiming to be another.[61]

Not only knowledge (and the world knowledge is about) and epistemology are constructed; we as embodied, knowing selves and as communities of such selves are also constructed—"stitched together imperfectly." What might seem an epistemological objectivist's nightmare is construed by feminists as the necessary starting point for talking about knowledge claims, which are, as feminists say, claims on people's lives. For feminists, objectivity is not about transcending limits and responsibility, but about apprehending embodied specificity and being answerable for what we learn to see and know.

Perhaps because women have been and are so frequently objectified, feminist epistemology lays great stress on a quite different disposition, one that regards the object of knowledge

> as an actor and agent, not a screen or a ground or a resource, never finally as a slave to the master that closes off the dialectic in his unique agency and authorship of "objective" knowledge.... [C]oming to terms with the agency of the '"objects" studied is the only way to avoid gross error and false knowledge of many kinds....[62]

"Coming to terms with the agency of the object of knowledge" also shows respect for the object; this is more a statement commending observer/subject humility vis-à-vis the surround than it is a glorification of the actor-agent/object. The disposition to regard the object as agent does entail risks—personal, epistemological, even political. It has a chance to work better if "conversation" replaces "discovery" as the key metaphor for knowledge-seeking. Such conversation involves sensitivity to relations of power and privilege that silence some voices and amplify others. It also involves commitment to participatory rather than coercive values. Among these values care (in the sense of both "carefulness" and "loving care") counts for a great deal: there is a kind of reliable, very elaborate specificity about the world (including other humans) that, if attended to with care, generates quite sturdy knowledge.[63] (It should but probably does not go without saying that subjectivity cannot help playing a role in the establishment of objectivity; that role, monitored self-consciously, is positive.)

Feminist thinkers argue that "objectivity" must cease to name the epistemological outcomes of a driving ambition to control or master the objects of knowledge. Instead it must be associated with the provisional, partial, and ongoing search for fidelity in and about a world, as Haraway points out, in which "'we' are permanently mortal, that is, not in 'final' control . . . ."[64] Attentive humility and answerability are two of the qualities most in demand for this sort of search.

6. *Accountability*

Accountability has been part of this discussion from the start. The whole project of feminist epistemologies arose from a profound dissatisfaction with the perceived unresponsiveness of traditional epistemological frameworks to "what women know," to "women's ways of knowing," and to issues of moment to women's lives but excluded from prevailing (androcentric) agendas in scientific research (both "hard" and "social") and philosophical/ethical reflection. Feminist discussion of traditional epistemological frameworks has judged them wanting in two ways. First, it has dealt with what might be called their "incompetence" to encompass or acknowledge a wider epistemological horizon—one that takes women, for example, into serious account. As Minnich points out, this incompetence was a "log" in the eyes of those who discerned the "motes" distorting others' vision: " . . . *the reasons why it was considered right and proper to exclude the majority of humankind were and are built into the very foundations of what was established as knowledge.*"[65] Any theory or way of talking about how we know must be "competent" to include the knowing of those (like women) who have been excluded.

Second, feminists have dealt with the injustices that flow from—or are at least fostered by—faulty epistemological frameworks. In doing so, they have given a particularly spirited series of accounts of the ethical and moral dimensions both of what we know and, at one level of abstraction removed, of the criteria we use to gather, test, legitimate, and pass along what we know. They have shown the intimate, reciprocal interrelation between the construction of knowledge and the construction of epistemologies, between what is "seen" and the lenses through which we look. Whatever the aesthetic or even intellectual merits of this sort of analysis (and there are some), feminists have been driven mainly by a conscientious awareness of the damage— physical, psychological, economic, spiritual, and other— exclusionary frameworks foster, and their commitment to changing such frameworks.[66] Even those who benefit from such frameworks are damaged by them, though not in the same ways or to the same degree.[67]

The point of distinguishing what is "incompetent" (in the sense used here) from what is wrong (because it generates injustice) is to establish both that there are two elements involved and that, while they can be distinguished, they cannot be separated. Code makes this quite explicit:

Every . . . process [of moral deliberation] has a cognitive core, for the quality of the deliberation and the conclusions—both theoretical and practical— it legitimates are shaped by an agent's *knowledge* of the situation, the problem, and the people

concerned . . . . [The] quality of the cognitive project
in which it is based shapes moral thought and
action . . . . [And] conversely, ethical issues are implicated in analyses of knowledge . . . .[68]

If this argument is valid, as most feminists would claim,
then to the extent that one accepts accountability for one
element, one must also accept it for the other.

But feminist epistemologists understand accountability
not only—or even primarily—as an individual (or collective)
moral burden "over against" intellectual or ethical standards
set for knowers, knowledge, and knowing, whether that
burden is borne by privileged men (who may exclude women),
or by relatively privileged women (who may also exclude
others). Epistemological accountability, feminists argue, is
rather—and mainly—interpersonal, a matter of going about
the tasks of scrutinizing frameworks, constructing alternatives,
examining consequences, legitimating epistemological evidence, and so forth " . . . in *shared* processes of discovery,
expression, interpretation, and adjustment *between persons.*"[69]

In lifting up the differences between knowing "objects"
and knowing people, Code seeks to illustrate the negotiated
(even more than the constructed) character of much of our
most highly valued knowledge as social and political creatures. " . . . [K]nowing other people," she writes, "precisely
because of the fluctuations and contradictions of subjectivity, is an ongoing, communicative, interpretive process."[70]
The reciprocity involved in this sort of knowing invites
accountability; when reciprocity is not recognized, nor accountability accepted, brute power fabricates what passes
for knowledge, and such knowledge need not be "competent" in the sense described above.

Interpersonal epistemological accountability is risky
business, for it requires ongoing involvement with others.
And

> [i]f the others I need to understand are actual
> others . . . and not . . . replaceable occupants of a
> general status, they will require of me an under-
> standing of their/our story and its concrete detail.
> Without this I cannot know *how it is* with others
> toward whom I will act . . . .[71]

The understanding "others" will require takes at least some
of its shape from the assumptions epistemological frameworks help us to sustain about what can be known, who
can know, and what knowledge is for as well as what it is
about. The fact that knowing in this interpersonal context
means knowing "actual others," not "replaceable occupants
of a general status," means that epistemological frameworks
must avoid what some feminists call "totalizing," that is,
acting as if one size assumption, criteria, or guideline is
appropriate to all. Uniformity and completeness, resolution
and stability, antidotes to the anxieties generated by their
mundane opposites, inspire totalizing theories in many disciplines, the sciences and philosophy among them.

Accountability in epistemological terms means embracing the notion that knowledge is a profoundly moral concern. It means acknowledging the range and richness of the
ways knowing and theories about it take moral shape. Finally, it means acting as if one is answerable, both individually and as a member of the larger human collectivity, for
one's approach to knowing.

7. *Turning to Luther*

Late twentieth-century feminists who have thought a lot
about knowing began to do so out of a passionate concern,
rooted in (their) lived experience, that traditional epistemologies nourished on power and privilege not only

underreport reality but also wreak havoc ethically. Feminists' constructive responses to the ignorance and abuses fostered by exclusionary theories about knowing stress greater sensitivity to the value and complexity of our various "lived experiences," individually and collectively. There are no "innocent" positions in the struggles to transform both ways of knowing and the reality that knowing refers to. A "strong objectivity" involves a provisional, partial, and ongoing search for fidelity within and about a world we do not, finally, control; in this search, we need to seek out multiple voices beginning, perhaps, with those whose voices have not yet been heard. This project requires accountability, not only to reliable standards of evidence but more important, to one another and a shared future.

At this juncture, I will risk asserting that as we turn from secular feminist philosophers and their twentieth-century epistemologies to Luther and his sixteenth-century theology of the cross, we may find intriguing affinities. I am less interested in spelling them out here—their collaboration is taken up in Chapter 3—than in suggesting that they are there, and in inviting the reader to meet a different kind of reformer: one whose life, disposition, and work are rich resources for a conversation we've wished we'd been able to have for years.

Luther's Theology
of the Cross

A t the end of April 1518, Martin Luther (1483–1546) pre-
sided at the opening disputation of Heidelberg's chapter of the Augustinian Order. Under debate was a series of
philosophical and theological theses, written by Luther, that
articulated some of the key components of his emerging
theological agenda. Theses 16 through 21 contained the
most important statements of what would come to be called
theologia crucis, or theology of the cross[1]:

16. The person who believes that he can obtain
    grace by doing what is in him adds sin to sin
    so that he becomes doubly guilty.
17. Nor does speaking in this manner give cause
    for despair, but for arousing the desire to
    humble oneself and seek the grace of Christ.
18. It is certain that man must utterly despair of
    his own ability before he is prepared to re-
    ceive the grace of Christ.
19. That person does not deserve to be called a
    theologian who looks upon the invisible things
    of God as though they were clearly percep-

tible in those things which have actually happened (Rom. 1:20).

20. He deserves to be called a theologian, however, who comprehends the visible and manifest things of God seen through suffering and
the cross.

21. A theologian of glory calls evil good and good
evil. A theologian of the cross calls the thing
what it actually is.[2]

The meaning and significance of these theses and the
theological framework they signal emerge more clearly if
they are understood as fruits of Luther's development as a
man, a biblical exegete, and a theologian. Occurring within
a politically and economically tumultuous historical period,
this development was woven into his long struggle with the
theological tradition of which he was a faithful part. Eventually, Luther would reject what he characterized in the
Heidelberg theses as a "theology of glory" and embrace
what he called the "theology of the cross."

From the beginning, however, Luther's struggle involved
much more than theological dissatisfaction. Personal piety,
the center of gravity in his life as a monk; the practices of
the church that shaped not only his vocation but also much
of social, political, and economic life in all Europe; and the
rich and often raucous intellectual debate among princes
and popes, humanists and heretics, were but a few of the
forces that incited and flavored Luther's initially private,
then professional, and then increasingly public—but always,
also, personal—reflection.

Scholars have long recognized the key role "experience" played in Luther's theology, whether as the medium
in which sinners despair of their own capacity to please
God or as the arena in which God's salvific initiative bears
fruit in and through the lives of the justified. What becomes
increasingly apparent as evidence accumulates, however, is

the driving role Luther's particular life experience plays in the unfolding of his thought. The enormous personal and professional risks he took "can certainly be understood only if one is aware how intensely he felt himself personally affected by his own struggle through the years . . . with the proper relationship of man toward God."[3]

There was an intimate relationship between what Luther lived as a historical subject, on the one hand, and what Luther said and wrote, on the other. " . . . [T]he study of Luther's life," writes Ebeling, "involves us to a greater degree than in the case of almost any other theologian with his person."[4] The life of Luther the theologian was the life of Luther the justified sinner and the life of Luther the outlaw and the life of Luther the university professor and the life of Katarina von Bora's husband. In all of those roles he made it clear that for him theology had most emphatically to do with his own and other people's *lives* before God and with one another. Theologizing is existential. Luther put it this way:

> Experience alone makes a theologian. . . . It is by living—no, rather it is by dying and being damned that a theologian is made, not by understanding, reading, or speculating.[5]

His words could have been a motto interpreting the whole of his life, Ebeling says. He adds that Luther's was "a theology . . . lived existentially."[6] This union of conceptual understanding and personal experience changed the course of his own life and had profound consequences for many others as well.

The following discussion, which draws on the work of widely recognized and respected Luther scholars, is intended as a sustainable description of rather than an argument about Luther's theology of the cross. These pages focus principally on the emergence and the functions of the *theologia crucis* in response to a problem Luther felt and perceived acutely, both personally and in more global terms.

Wrestling with Iustitia Dei

"At the beginning of the sixteenth century," writes Owen Chadwick, "everyone that mattered in the Western Church was crying out for reformation."[7] The church—indeed, all Europe—had been undergoing a long-term upheaval, not only morally and politically but also spiritually and theologically. Diverse ecclesiastical movements "sought to revitalize the church, to rescue it from signs of decadence, to purify it of abuses, to disconnect it from economic interests and political powers."[8] According to Chadwick, however, few who clamored for reform believed that theology or church doctrine was at the heart of what needed to be altered.

Against this backdrop, Martin Luther arrived on the campus of the relatively new but up-and-coming university at Wittenberg in 1512, not as a man of destiny, mysterious and lonely, armed with a clearly formulated, new and "true" theology, and filled with a sense of divine mission for reforming the church, but rather as a late-medieval theologian and biblical scholar, very much of his time. Luther began his career as professor of Bible at Wittenberg during the winter semester of 1513–1514, a year after he received his degree as a doctor of theology from the same institution. His first lectures (or at least the first that are preserved) were on the Psalms. Between 1513 and 1521, he then lectured on Romans, Galatians, Hebrews, and the Psalms again. (He may also have lectured on Titus and on Judges; no texts or notes of these lectures exist.)

The young professor's knowledge of Scripture was prodigious and intimate; he came to know much of the Bible from memory. First as a monk, then as a student, and finally as a preacher and teacher, he pored over the biblical texts, in Latin and then in Greek (using a new translation by Erasmus, issued in 1516); he also learned Hebrew in order to listen to and interrogate Old Testament texts more carefully.[9] As was customary, Luther used biblical commentaries by the scholastic scholars and the church fathers, of whom the most significant for Luther was Augustine on Romans.

His disposition toward Scripture was, Martin Brecht writes,

> characterized by a willingness to listen intensively to the text. It was anything but detached and uninvolved. . . . [I]t was not just one's reason that had to be involved, but also one's emotion. . . . [Luther] liked to speak about "ruminating" on the word of the Bible[,] . . . a meditating which existentially confronts the text, or rather lets oneself be confronted by it. . . . The way the Scripture spoke became . . . the critical norm against which he measured the theology of his time.[10]

Scholastics' theologizing became odious to Luther at least in part because he was convinced that their approach, far from engaging the word of God as it lay open to humankind in the pages of the Bible, distanced theologians and those they taught from the God who spoke through the texts.

As he persevered in his study of Scripture, Ebeling writes that Luther "came to be increasingly scandalized by what he was taught . . . ," namely, that

> . . . the grace infused in the first place in baptism, and renewed after each mortal sin in the sacrament of penance, inhered in the person who received it as a new supernatural faculty enabling him to live a saintly life, even though still imperfectly. Thus grace ultimately cast man back upon himself.[11]

In contrast, Luther found in the texts of the Psalms a God-
sent truth that confirmed his own experience

> ... that a man always falls short of God's de-
> mand, always remains a sinner, or—even worse—
> that he does not acknowledge his situation before
> God, and rather what he wants to offer God is
> precisely his own pious acts.[12]

His own monkish attempt to live a holy and perfect life
before God failed miserably and repeatedly, throwing him
into despair.

At the heart of the theological crisis that afflicted the
church lay the doctrine of justification. The significance of
the doctrine of justification, according to McGrath, has to do
with the centrality in the Christian faith of the teaching

> that reconciliation has been effected between
> God and sinful man through Jesus Christ. . . .
> [J]ustification is primarily concerned with the ques-
> tion of how this saving action may be appropri-
> ated by the individual. . . . The hope of salvation . . .
> lends particular urgency to the question . . . : [w]hat
> [must] man . . . do . . . to be saved?[13]

During the last part of the fifteenth century, many faithful
people debated this urgent question. Despite a great deal of
highly nuanced discourse on the subject, however, the lack
of clear official church teaching on the question of justification sowed confusion among both the devout faithful and
the professional theologians of the church, and helped set
the conditions leading to outright rebellion, beginning in
the second decade of the sixteenth century.

As a theologian of the church and (not insignificantly)
because he longed for certainty about his own standing
before God, Luther appears to have focused much of his

attention on the doctrine of justification, especially during
the years between 1509 and 1519. Like many of his late-
medieval theological counterparts, Luther's understanding of
justification was shaped by the *via moderna,* according to
which God justified sinful human beings, not on the basis
of their own merits, but rather on the basis of *iustitia Dei,*
or the righteousness of God, understood to be divine faith-
fulness within the order of salvation God had ordained.
God's part in this divinely established covenant was to judge
all sinners justly and equitably, that is, to judge all persons
on the basis of how they lived their lives, not on the basis
of their status in society.

But what could ensure that this God would justify a
given sinner? Such a sinner would have to have some quality,
satisfy some criterion, to hold up his or her end of the
"bargain" God had established. Under the terms of the pact,
all sinners were expected to do *quod en se est,* or "what was
in them"—or what they could—to merit God's gracious
justifying action. God had promised that grace would not be
denied to those who complied with their part of the deal.
Grace was God's helping hand, the "leg up" every struggling human creature needed, in his or her striving toward
God. Like many of the faithful, Luther—sinner and theologian—was tortured by the thought that there might be something "that was in him" to do that he had neglected to do
and that God would therefore not grant him grace. Even
before Luther entered the monastery in 1505[14] he had
struggled with the problem of how to find not only a
righteous, but a merciful God.

Luther's relentless existential and theological struggle
with this problem may have been aggravated by his particular psychological problems[15] or spiritual scrupulosity; the
point is interesting but not critical. What is important is that
what made the elusiveness of God's mercy *the* problem for
Luther, as for countless others of his time, was his abject
sense of failure either to deserve or to be able to earn that

mercy. Such a sense of failure, in turn, was shaped as much by the church's understanding of how humans could and should approach this problem as it was by any other factor. Sinners *could* appropriate God's grace, the church taught: Acknowledging and accepting God's eye-opening judgment on one's own lame protestation of righteousness produced sufficient contrition and humility to warrant God's forgiving grace. Sinners had only to confess their sins in order to be minimally worthy. Not only were they capable of doing so, the church (and only the church) also provided the means to do so. In the celebration of the sacraments (by priests), God's grace became available.

As a monk, Luther confessed and confessed . . . and confessed, until in exasperation, his superior, Johann Staupitz, told him he should commit some really serious sins that would be worthy of forgiveness, instead of the trivial offenses for which he constantly sought absolution. "[E]ven when he had done the most rigorous of good works," William Hordern writes, Luther despaired, fearing that

> his motivation for doing them was self-centered. He was not acting because he loved God with all of his heart and mind and strength, he was acting because he wanted to save Martin Luther's eternal soul. He was serving God because it was good for himself.[16]

Even acts and vows involving self-denial—among them fasting, celibacy, and poverty—which formed such a key part of monastic practice, seemed self-serving. Luther later characterized this human disposition toward self rather than toward God as *incurvatus in se ipsum* (turned in on oneself).[17]

The medieval church provided a seemingly never-ending stream of "products," in addition to confession, the purchase (e.g., indulgences) or practice (e.g., pilgrimages) of which might demonstrate the desire of a believer to do that "extra little something" in him or her, made realizable by a kind of ecclesial "technology" of grace. There was always one more thing . . . . Given that sinners could avail themselves of God's grace, they were then also responsible to do so; those who did not were derelict, and (likely) damned. But the theology of the *via moderna* provided no reassurance, even to the conscientious: " . . . [T]he medieval theological tradition . . . was unanimous [that] man simply cannot know with certainty whether he is worthy of hate or love by God.[18] For sinners as conscience-stricken as Luther was, the failure to gain the assurance of God's grace, even through the many means available (not least of all, in the practice of the monk's vocation), had the effect of reinforcing the power of the church's thought and practices, and of deepening the fears that failure to respond to the means of grace engendered.[19]

If Luther continued to live under the shadow of the wrathful, righteous God, he found little comfort in the *via moderna*'s understanding of the role of Christ. Christ functioned as lawgiver rather than as redeemer; the law he gave was the "law of Christ," or of love, but it *was* law, not gospel. Christ's role in helping the sinner was confined to providing instruction and example in responding to the demands of the law. Sinners were still required to fulfill the vague and ultimately unverifiable demand—to do *quod en se est.*

The key to the transformation of Luther's understanding of justification and the origins of the theology of the cross seems to lie in his long struggle, played out with special forcefulness between 1509 and 1519, when he lectured on the Psalms and on Romans, with the question of what is meant by "the righteousness of God," or *iustitia Dei.* How could a God characterized by the sort of *iustitia* according to which each person receives what he or she is entitled to, justify sinners? How could the idea of a "righteous God" be good news to any sinner? Even if divine justice were understood more broadly (as it was by theologians of the *via moderna*), as residing in the covenant God had originally established with humankind, through which sinners could be justified if they did "what they could," what sinner could ever be sure to have done everything possible? Even this more ample interpretation of *iustitia Dei* provided little assurance.

According to his own testimony, Luther's voyage of theological discovery had a deeply personal, existential character. In a preface the reformer contributed to a 1545 Latin edition of his works, he recalled his intense struggle with Paul more than a quarter century earlier. Despite his "great desire to understand St. Paul in his letter to the Romans," Luther wrote, he had been confounded by "that one phrase in the first chapter [v. 17]: 'The righteousness of God is revealed in it [the gospel].' " Having learned to understand *iustitia Dei* as "the formal or active righteousness . . . , by which God is righteous, and punishes unrighteous sinners," this scholarly, faithful monk could not decipher in this biblical passage any God-sent good news meant for him. "I drove myself mad, with a desperate disturbed conscience," he writes, "persistently pounding upon Paul in this passage. . . . "

"God being merciful," Luther noted, the resolution finally did come:

> I began to understand that "righteousness of God" as that by which the righteous lives by the gift of God, namely by faith, and this sentence, "the righteousness of God is revealed," to refer to a passive righteousness, by which the merciful God justifies us by faith.

These same words—"the righteousness of God"—that had caused Luther such anguish, even hatred of God, were transformed; he felt, he wrote, "as though I had been born again, and . . . this passage in Paul became the very gate of paradise for me."[20]

Luther had wrestled through several stages in his understanding of the righteousness of God. Initially, God's righteousness was a demanding, even wrathful, justice, before which a person might stand on the basis of his or her own good works and the forgiving grace of God, very much in keeping with the *via moderna* view. Gradually, Luther came to believe that "[a]ll that was required of man was that he humbled himself before God, in order that he might receive the gift of grace which God would then bestow upon him," a position, McGrath argues, that was also "firmly set within a well-established medieval theological tradition."[21] It was not clear whether humility or faith was the righteousness God demanded of sinners in order to transform and justify them with God's own righteousness. Finally, Luther identified God's judgment and God's righteousness; the sinner, driven by God's own initiative to realize his or her own unworthiness and cling to God's mercy, stood before God, cloaked in the righteousness of God: Christ. Through the three stages, human initiative diminished, then vanished; God's initiative took over entirely.[22]

As long as sinners tried to draw a false analogy between *iustitia* as humans conceptualized it and *iustitia* as God worked it out salvifically,[23] they would continue to believe that they might secure their own justification before God by their own moral efforts. Luther could see nothing in human concepts of *iustitia* that corresponded to *iustitia Dei*. Human concepts of righteousness, Luther came to believe, were utterly inadequate to describe the standing of human beings before God (*coram Deo*). Once sinners recognized this, they were driven to despair of their self-saving pretensions; they were driven to the only "righteousness of God" that, *coram Deo*, did justify: faith in Christ who *is* the "righteousness of God." Only when the sinner appreciated the distinction between human and divine concepts of *iustitia* did justification become a real possibility. Faith in Christ (*fides Christi*), far from being an accomplishment of the repentant sinner, was itself a gift from God. Through it, the sinner did not *become* righteous, as Augustine had held; rather, the *iustitia Christi aliena*, or "alien righteousness of Christ," "covered" the sinner *coram Deo.*

The entire person was justified; the entire person remained a sinner. In keeping with his understanding of humans as holistic creatures, Luther held "that 'flesh' (*caro*) and 'spirit' (*spiritus*) are not to be regarded as man's lower and higher faculties . . . but . . . as descriptions of the whole person considered under different aspects."[24] A person viewed from the aspect of flesh was seen in terms of his or her egoism and alienation from God; the same person viewed from the aspect of the spirit was seen in his or her openness to God and God's promises. Luther explicated theologically what seemed clear to him existentially: The sinner is both *iustus et peccator simul.*[25] Through the "alien righteousness of Christ"—that is, a righteousness extrinsic to human creatures—the person was righteous before God; intrinsically, that same person was still a sinner.

Luther's proposals concerning *iustitia Dei* underscored the radical dichotomy between human and divine concepts of *iustitia* and expressed Luther's conviction that even the righteousness of faith was God's work rather than a human *quod in se est,* aimed at eliciting God's saving response. As we have seen, Luther was tortured by the possibility that sinners could "qualify" themselves to receive God's justifying grace by doing "what was in them," a notion he then rejected, together with its more subtle but equally pernicious variant: that sinners could dispose themselves to be justified by God if they humbled, or humiliated, themselves adequately.

The key for Luther was the assertion that "it is *God* who takes the initiative in justification. It [was] not man who humbled *himself*—it [was] *God* who humble[d] him."[26] Sinners, experiencing God's wrath, recognized that they could not by themselves qualify for mercy; they had to concede that left to their own devices they were entirely unworthy, "unqualified," to come before God. Luther used the term *opus alienum Dei*, God's alien work, to describe this divine initiative that empowered sinners, in faith, to throw themselves helplessly and hopelessly on God's mercy—and, by means of what Luther called *opus proprium Dei*, "God's proper work," they received it. As he explained in the Heidelberg theses, "Thus an action which is alien to God's nature results in a deed belonging to his very nature: he makes a person a sinner so that he may make him righteous."[27] There is, then, a dialectic between God's "alien" work and God's "proper" work. The one was the means by which the other was accomplished. The one occurred through, because of, in connection with, the other. One could not be comprehended without reference to the other.

Underlying the formulation of the notions of *opus alienum Dei* and *opus proprium Dei* was the full and sufficient and, from the standpoint of human understanding, mysterious agency of God in justification. The point, finally, was not *how* God justified the sinner; the point was, it was *God* who justified. This was utterly critical, in Luther's view; in one form and another, through hundreds of years and at least as many finely drawn proposals, theologians had obscured that central, gospel truth. Unless human salvation was not dependent upon human effort, it could not be certain:

> To know God means to know what God can and does do, not his power and his potentialities, but his power as it is actually at work in everything that exists. . . . But if man has to know, for the sake of his salvation and his certainty, what he is capable of with regard to his salvation, then he evidently knows neither what he is capable of,

nor what God is, until he knows for certain that he can *do nothing* towards his salvation. And that very inability permits him to be certain of salvation, which is based upon the act of God alone.[28]

The Emergence of the Theologia Crucis

Luther scholars express the centrality of the cross in Luther's theology in a variety of ways. Paul Althaus, for example, declares that for Luther, " . . . the cross of Christ is the standard by which all genuine theology is measured . . ."; the *theologia crucis* is the "essence of true theology."[29] According to Walther von Loewenich, "For Luther the cross is not only the subject of theology; it is the distinctive mark of all theology. . . . The cross of Christ is . . . the center that provides perspective for all theological statements."[30] And McGrath observes, "For Luther, Christian thinking about God comes to an abrupt halt at the foot of the cross. The Christian is forced . . . [either to] seek God elsewhere, or . . . [to] make the cross itself the foundation and criterion of his thought about God."[31] These commentators are restating Luther's own often-quoted dictum: *Crux sola est nostra theologia,* or "the cross alone is our theology."[32]

But the transition from Luther's struggle with and insights about the righteousness of God to his *theologia crucis* is neither simple nor linear, not least of all in view of the fact that Luther did not himself develop a systematic exposition of the theology of the cross, as a number of twentieth-century scholars have done.[33] There is no reason to believe that Luther escaped what he identified as the troubling impact of the cross on the language, thought, and spirit of theology. What is critical is to acknowledge that in these insights, as in others, Luther—like other theologians, then and now—was struggling to articulate what he himself was learning: both about what he believed was profoundly out of sync with the gospel as well as what he believed came closer to its truths.

His writing is rather like the journal of a sixteenth-century sea captain passing through unknown seas on a great voyage of exploration: It is filled with all the available technical expertise needed to navigate along with the passion to discover; it is also colored by the restlessness of the not-having-arrived, the disquiet of the given uncertainties of the enterprise, the acknowledgment of the utter centrality of faith in the journeying. That is to say, Luther's insights did not translate into a safe theological berth, a place which, having arrived there, would give him peace of mind and a quiet, untroubled life. To have had the insight was not to have gained justification; to have glimpsed the truth, if that is what it was, was not to have gained what neither reason nor good works had ever gained—as far as he could discern.[34]

Luther's struggles with the spiritual reality and the theological concept of the righteousness of God contained a preview of the theology of the cross. His affirmation of justification as initiated and carried out by God alone both distinguished him increasingly from his contemporaries and compelled him to draw entirely new consequences for the whole theological enterprise that engaged him.[35] Not least of all, his struggles re-ignited the God question. What sort of God is this, who in righteousness justifies the ungodly? How are we to think about this God?

Luther's movement from the righteousness of God to the theology of the cross involves a descriptive and an intellectual shift: While there is certainly new substance to Luther's theology of the cross, it also, and perhaps even more emphatically, can be characterized as a new way of "doing" theology. These two aspects cannot be separated.

If "logic" may be understood as the sequence of steps of theological reasoning needed to get from "here" to "there,"

then the logic of the movement from Luther's new appre-
hension of *iustitia Dei* to the theology of the cross is fairly
clear to describe. Once Luther had come to believe that
God was the sole agent and initiator of justification, and
that the "righteousness of God" was the "passive righteousness with which God makes the sinner righteous," he asked,
How does God do this? *Where* is this righteousness to be
found? His eventual response was to yet another—and, finally,
the most precise—question, namely, *Who* is the righteousness of God? And he found the clearest answer in Paul's
epistle to the Romans: Christ is our righteousness.[36]

There is another sort of logic at work, too, a logic that
confounds what is normally thought to be "logical." Beginning with his radical new understanding of the righteousness of God, Luther rejected what had been a sturdy
methodological approach in theology, that is, the assumption that theological language was reliably analogical. While
certainly not entirely congruent with its object, this assumption went, human talk about God bore some reasonable
and discernible relation to it. But if the righteousness of
God, that "passive righteousness" with which God clothes
us, is Christ; if it is God who acts and not sinners who
bargain with God; if it is, finally, God who is crucified, then
analogical language and the reasoning on which it is based
are simply not adequate.[37]

Human reason's power to know who and what God is,
is suspended, its scholastic powers nullified. And now, Luther
argued, the cross required that all theological talk be recast
in a new, cross-shaped syntax. The one who learned to
theologize in terms of the cross, with its reversal of the
expected, the preconceived, would discover "that man lives
in theological twilight, in a world of half-light and half-
truths."[38]

The contrast between the "righteousness of God" and
human notions of "righteousness" could not be greater. The
suffering of Christ upon the cross, and his apparent aban-

donment by God, express God's judgment on human understandings of strength, wisdom, and justice. How could
this be God's righteousness, this pathetic human being caught
up in the weakness, the folly, and the injustice of an appalling crucifixion spectacle? This was more than a dichotomy
between human and divine judgment; according to Luther,
this was God's way of frustrating the pretenses of human
reason and judgment:

> It is therefore called the judgment of God . . . ,
> because it is contrary to the judgment of men . . . ,
> condemning what men choose, and choosing what
> men condemn. And this judgment has been shown
> to us in the cross of Christ.[39]

The cross confounds the powers of human reason to make
sense of it.

God's works, Luther argued—like God's righteousness,
God's wisdom, God's glory—are hidden in the form of their
opposite (*sub contrario suo abscondita sunt*), and the cross
is the ultimate instantiation of this apparent paradox. In his
lectures on the Psalms, Luther quoted the passage in the
first chapter of I Corinthians concerning the "word of the
cross"[40]:

> . . . God chose what is foolish in the world to
> shame the wise; God chose what is weak in the
> world to shame the strong; God chose what is
> low and despised in the world, things that are
> not, to reduce to nothing things that are (vv. 27–
> 28).[41]

The central insight of Luther's *theologia crucis* was that
God is revealed in the cross of Christ. Any attempt to seek
God elsewhere will fail. McGrath clarifies the difficulty of
this insight:

> ... [T]here is a radical discontinuity between the *empirically perceived situation* and the *situation as discerned by faith*. To the eye of reason, all that can be seen in the cross is a man dying in apparent weakness and folly, under the wrath of God. If God *is* revealed in the cross, he is not recognisable as *God*. ... Reason ... deduces that God cannot be present in the cross ... , as the perceived situation in no way corresponds to the preconceived situation.[42]

A theologian of glory, Luther argued, expects God to look powerful, mighty, beautiful, radiant, glorious—in a word, God-like. Certainly the appalling spectacle of crucifixion outside the city walls is not. Only to the eye of faith, Luther would respond, would God's self-revelation on the cross become plain. Human reason might be capable of forming a general idea of God's attributes, but it could not break through to apprehend God's intention toward humans or know the meaning of God's activity "for us" (*pro nobis*) worked out through the cross.[43]

And what is faith? Luther appropriated the definition given in Hebrews 11:1: "Faith has to do with things not seen." Faith is neither sight (as in "seeing is believing") nor triumphant confidence. "The certitude of faith," Hall writes of Luther's understanding, "is not a matter of demonstration or success, but a matter of trust ... in the promise of a God who gives life to the dead and brings into existence the things that are not (Rom., ch. 4)."[44] For Luther, that trust is experienced, can be experienced, only in relation to what cannot be seen or grasped by human understanding—that is, God—at the point at which one becomes utterly clear about one's own incapacity to "have" God on one's own terms or one's own merits. "That faith and God belong together is the theology of the cross," Ebeling writes, "a theology not based on human wishes, but upon the will of God."[45]

Functions of the Theology of the Cross

Having made this historical sketch of Luther's theology of the cross, let us now turn to an interpretation of this theology in terms of at least three functions: critique, announcement, and equip-ment.

Critique

Luther's theology of the cross was a critique leveled against the official theology of his day. But the critique went deeper than theology.

Luther made quite clear his critical intention when, in the Heidelberg disputation theses, he contrasted the "theologian of the cross" with the "theologian of glory."[46] ". . . [T]hose who were 'theologians' and still were called fools by the Apostle [Paul] in Rom. 1 [:22] . . . ," he declared in the explanations to Theses 19 and 20,

> . . . misused the knowledge of God through works. . . . Now it is not sufficient for anyone, and it does him no good to recognize God in his glory and majesty, unless he recognizes him in the humility and shame of the cross.[47]

The results of the work of such "theologians," Luther firmly held, were clear to behold: the Roman church, for example, was a political and economic power that among other things traded without apology in the "paper" of forgiveness, namely, indulgences. The intellectual authors of such rampant practical "misuses of the knowledge of God," Luther was persuaded, were the scholastic thinkers, whose powerful philosophical and theological assumptions and arguments underwrote the very notion that sinners could bargain with God and come out ahead.

The moralism and religious intellectualism of the church and the scholastic method both reflected and fostered something Luther understood as even more basic, something he targeted over and over again in his theologizing.[48] Humans, he contended, believe and act as if they have the power to invent, name, describe, control, and dispense God.[49] This god, however, is a god of their own choosing, bearing no resemblance to God who creates and redeems them by a power that is God's alone. The god humans invent can be found wherever (human) glory, majesty, and power are most evident, whether on the scale of the institutional church or of the individual human heart.

For Luther the relationship between God and humankind was bedrock, not only for the activity of theologians but, more profoundly, for the daily life and practice of each person. This relationship was the framework of meaning, that which ordered and organized human existence: not only in terms of its ultimate destiny but also in all its concrete, daily, detailed dimensions. Humans inevitably fail to be clear about the true nature and character of this relationship, and especially about God's purpose for and way with humans. It is not simply that humans could, if they wanted to, make an honest attempt and might succeed in it; to the contrary, they cannot help calling things by their wrong names. "A theologian of glory," Luther wrote, "calls evil good and good evil." Specifically, he explains, "they call the good of the cross evil and the evil of a deed good."[50] It does not get more basic than that.

Humans' constitutional proclivity for misnaming is rooted in the brokenness the Christian tradition associates with the Fall, an estrangement from God whose completeness is such that humans are not even aware of the extent of its impact. From the human point of view (*coram hominibus*), it is as if the framework for the reality within which humans live and move has fractured. At the most fundamental level— the sense a person has of who he or she is—this fractured framework produces an entirely distorted self-portrait. Relationships with others are equally distorted. The sense of who one is in relation to and with God—which gives shape and form to everything about one, within oneself and in relation to others—is out of reach.

Luther's concern was not to condemn human nature, humans' willful ignorance of God, and its fateful consequences. Nor was Luther's aim to prescribe a "better way," a remedy for the human condition that might be within reach of those who awoke to their plight. To prescribe would (and does) give credence to the insidious fractured framework just depicted. He was, rather, passionately concerned to *describe* the situation in which humans are, whether they "find themselves" in this situation or not (left to their own devices, they will not).[51]

Luther meant to underscore the point that humans cannot avoid being governed by their own profoundly flawed framework, as long as they seek to "govern" themselves. He argued in scores of situations, to men and women of every station, about events and institutions and doctrines and politics and a host of other activities of daily living. The compulsion humans have to rely on and reside in their own power, Luther would say, is not abstract; it always takes concrete forms. This is what makes it so pernicious. There is evidence of it on every hand and in every form.

Luther vilified the church in Rome, headed by the pope, as the concrete ecclesiastic form such human triumphalism took. Selling indulgences to finance the redecoration of St. Peter's was not merely burdensome to Germans and unethical insofar as the sales focused on the salvation of souls and omitted mention of the Pope's financial straits; it was pernicious because it allowed and even encouraged people to believe that by paying money for a piece of parchment they could stand less uneasily before God. It allowed those who bought indulgences also to buy into the deadly myth that God, though greater by far, was on the whole not so different from the powerful of this world—who, for their part, were generally willing for that impression to go unchallenged.

Theologically, Luther identified a particularly virulent strain of the reliance of humans on their own power with those who purveyed a theology of glory, who preferred "works to suffering, glory to the cross, strength to weakness, wisdom to folly, and, in general, good to evil."[52] The cross of Jesus Christ was for Luther the fulcrum that stood on its head the human vision of God and of reality that underlay this theology, and the theology of the cross was the attempt the "friends of the cross," as Luther called them, made in faith to call things what they are. The cross confounds human expectations utterly: human expectations, most of all, of a God of might and majesty, of power and glory, whom the powerful generate out of the imagination of their hearts.

The cross is "an offence to the present world," writes Paul Fiddes.

> By choosing to reveal himself fully in a crucified man God contradicts all notions of what it means to be "divine"; by becoming weak and a prey to death God makes foolish the wisdom of this world which understands power to be the ability to inflict suffering, or at least to escape from it.[53]

In Luther's view, such a complete reversal of what "works" *coram mundo*—not only theologically, but existentially—could and did occur only through the event of the cross. The reversal, which affects every single dimension of human life, is the expression of God's graciousness *pro nobis*, the divine disposition we cannot apprehend or appropriate without the cross and the faith it makes possible, because it is only there that the hidden God becomes visible. "Hence," Luther wrote, "in order that there may be room for faith, it is necessary that everything which is believed should be hidden. It cannot, however, be more deeply hidden than under an object, perception, or experience which is contrary to it."[54] At the foot of the cross, then, the power of philosophical speculation and moral striving—human works—comes to a full stop, forfeiting any claim to produce or to reflect knowledge of God.

A comment on reason. Luther's unbridled attacks on human reason are almost legendary, though they are also well documented. This same Luther, as a careful scholar and skilled lecturer and debater, also praised reason extravagantly and often. Not surprisingly, Luther's apparent ambivalence about reason resolves in light of his larger theological program.

Reason, Luther believed, was a God-given gift which, when exercised within its proper limits, served with distinction. "In temporal affairs . . . the rational man is self-sufficient: here he needs no other light than reason's. Therefore, God does not teach us in the Scriptures how to build houses, make clothing . . . and the like. . . . " However, Luther continued, a critical distinction must be made:

> . . . [I]n godly affairs, that is, in those which have to do with God . . . —*here* . . . nature is absolutely stone-blind . . . [and] all of its conclusions are utterly false, as surely as God lives.[55]

This is to say that "natural reason," used within its proper domain—to draw logical conclusions, for example, or in human cultural endeavors—is an excellent gift. But reason has limits, and they were quite meaningful for Luther. When reason trespassed upon the domain of faith, or began to function metaphysically as the foundation of a world view, it went awry.[56] It was human reason that wanted to create a theology of glory, one that reflected humans' "reasonable" inferences about God and humankind and their relationship

to one another, inferences that ran exactly contrary to what
Luther had in mind in the theology of the cross.

Reason begins with itself, and orients everything to
itself. It begins with humans' approach to God, rather than
with God's initiative vis-à-vis humankind. Reason seeks to
understand God based on what can be discovered about
God from the world and the powers of human speculation,
bypassing God's incarnated revelation: Jesus in the manger
and on the cross. Perhaps most poignantly, the legalistic
religion reason generates cannot comprehend the Gospel's
message of free forgiveness by grace alone. It holds that a
just and holy God can be approached only by just and holy
people. Such legalism is "based upon a false inference,"
Gerrish writes.

> It is clear . . . that God's character is such that He
> requires His children to perform "good works",
> but reason quite wrongly infers that works are
> therefore required *for salvation itself*. . . . [O]ur
> acceptance with God does not depend upon our
> ability to satisfy him with good works: on the
> contrary, our ability to perform good works de-
> pends on our first being accepted by God, for He
> is the source of all goodness.[57]

Reason, Luther held, knows that good should be pro-
moted and evil avoided; but it does not know what is good
and what is evil. Reason knows that humans have moral
obligations, but it is not clear what the substance of those
obligations might be. Its grip on reality is formal, not rooted.
Philosophy, reason's playground and the underpinning of
the church's theology of glory,

> has no ear for the groaning and sighing that run
> through nature . . . . It knows nothing of a need for
> deliverance . . . . Just as the theology of glory

prefers works to sufferings, glory to the cross, power to weakness, . . . so philosophy would rather investigate the essences and actions of the creatures than listen to their groanings and expectations.[58]

Reason, when left to its own devices, cannot respond to the "troubled conscience" of the one who stands before God in fear; reason will continue to insist on calling "good evil and evil good."

Announcement

Luther's theology of the cross is not only critique; it also announces, in the language of faith, the way of God with humankind, a way that has profound implications for Christian life and theology.

What did Luther mean when he wrote of "the good of the cross"? He meant, first of all, that the suffering and death of the Son on the cross were utterly necessary events in God's salvific initiative for humankind. This occurred in at least two senses: Theologically, God effectuated the reconciliation of the world to Godself through the suffering, death, and resurrection of the Son. Epistemologically, the event of the cross confounds all human attempts to negotiate with a god invented in a human—a "reasonable"—image.[59] In bringing these attempts to nothing, the cross prepares humans to throw themselves instead, in faith (" . . . faith whereby one makes his own mind captive to the word of the cross . . . "[60]), on the mercy of the One who can be trusted to justify and save. God is acknowledged to be God. The theology of the cross means to shed some light on these acts of God as they affect those whose lives they were and are aimed to redeem; it does not claim to explain these acts.

What, then, is the "good of the cross"? In the most immediate sense, it is the event through which God acts to justify sinners.

Further reflection in light of Luther's thought reveals that the good of the cross lends itself to even more ample interpretation. In the explanation Luther provided for the twentieth thesis of the Heidelberg disputation, he wrote:

> So, also, in John 14 [:8], where Philip spoke according to the theology of glory: "Show us the Father." Christ forthwith set aside his flighty thought about seeking God elsewhere and led him to himself, saying, "Philip, he who has seen me has seen the Father" [John 14:9]. For this reason true theology and recognition of God are in the crucified Christ.[61]

For Luther it was not God's metaphysical attributes—at least one of the concerns of theologians of glory—that mattered to the person who seeks salvation; rather, it was God's intention for and toward humankind, that is, God's "personal" nature and activity. These are fully revealed only in the human Jesus. "We [humans] know how God thinks about us and how he relates to us," writes Althaus,

> only in the earthly reality of someone who is like us, that is, in the human will and activity of Jesus. For this reason, the primary and only saving truth is that God himself is present for us in the humanity of Jesus Christ.[62]

The "good of the cross" is that God has become incarnate in the human Jesus, whose life—given the brokenness of reality—led to the cross. God cannot be seen or grasped anywhere else. Precisely and only the life and death of the human Jesus provide a glimpse into God's heart, God's disposition toward humankind.

Hordern makes a direct connection between the theology of the cross and Luther's passionate emphasis on the revelation of God in the human Jesus. "For Luther," he writes,

> the theology of the cross is not simply a way of looking at Jesus' death. The actual crucifixion of Jesus is the culmination of what is involved in the whole of his life. The cross illustrates the way of God with humanity. . . . Because Jesus is the revelation of God, the theology of the cross describes the nature of God. By coming to the world in the human suffering form of Jesus, God is revealed as one who loves and suffers with humanity.[63]

For Luther *this* was salve for the troubled conscience.[64]

God's self-revelation, then, does not come in majesty, apprehended by the power of human reason, mediated by the power of the church. It does not come as a brilliant concept, a sublime abstraction, a reasonable inference or deduction. It comes, rather—unexpectedly—incarnate: in the "concreteness," the bodiliness, of the life experience of Jesus as a man among the men and women of his time. God's self-revelation does not come in glory and triumph, to the manor born, above the human fray. It appears instead as a defenseless baby, born in a dusty shed amid the inhospitableness of a town crowded with too many transients, and as a man who suffers, early and later, the consequences of the creatures' negation of the will of the Creator.

> As a result of . . . total immersion into the situation of human sin, [Jesus] is brought to the cross by human hands, and . . . suffers the forsakenness that is the natural consequence of broken human lives. . . . Looked at from the human perspective, we experience God as the one who sympathises

with us, and so we are enabled to face up both
to judgement and to acceptance.[65]

Unexpectedly, too, humankind experiences God's gracious
solidarity. Jesus opens a window on God's heart, allowing
humankind to know God's commitment to the world.[66]

A comment on experience. The practices of the Roman
church, backed by scholastic theology, sought to provide
assurances that the sinner could meet God halfway by doing
quod in se est. Such assurances simply contradicted Luther's
lived experience, which persuaded him of the utter
unreliability of both scholastic speculation and moral reasoning to guide him in relationship with God.[67] His troubled
conscience, he wrote years after the fact, drove him both to
distraction and deeper into Scripture, where he eventually
found in Paul the words that opened for him the "gates of
paradise."

Althaus observes that "experience is one of the principles" of Luther's theology. While it is "not a source of
knowledge in and by itself, . . . it definitely is a medium
through which knowledge is received."[68] For Luther it
was the gathering place for spiritual and theological "information" of every kind. In his own development, lived
experience played an utterly central role, and he accorded it a deeply theological significance. In his 1521
commentary on the Magnificat, for example, he called
experience the "school" of the Holy Spirit. "No one,"
Luther wrote,

> can correctly understand God or His Word unless
> he has received such understanding immediately
> from the Holy Spirit. But no one can receive it
> from the Holy Spirit without experiencing, prov-
> ing, and feeling it.[69]

That is to say, God works through and in the medium of human experience. "As the Word appeared in the human life of Jesus in a purely human setting," Hordern observes, "so the Holy Spirit is manifested in and through the purely human experience."[70]

Luther's emphasis on experience was "directed against a faith that is solely a concern of the mind."[71] As we have seen, Luther would have no commerce with the speculative theology of the scholastics. What sets "experience" at odds with speculation is its concreteness and its particularity; experience is neither abstract nor general—at least, not for purposes of Luther's theology, any more than it is for purposes of God's justifying work.

What sort of "experience" was Luther talking about? His own, surely; what he observed of others', very likely; and particularly that of the psalmists and Paul as they were recorded in biblical texts that Luther resonated with in their accounts of the experience of the individual before God.[72] In any case, experience was unsettling, complicated, fraught. A theologian of the cross, Luther asserted, was one who regarded reality from a standpoint radically different from that of a theologian of glory, a standpoint established by the self-revelation of God in the place of suffering, not in the place of power. For "friends of the cross," Luther also believed, the "true *Christian life* is not a life of *securitas*, lived out in the midst of a world in which the triumph of the good is assured,"[73] a world in which one could count on the coincidence of faith and fortune. The experience of friends of the cross is to live in the world as it is, without illusions. In the face of real life, faith (understood not as spiritual self-confidence but as utter trust in God's promise) is challenged over and over again, not only by what we see but by how we interpret what we see. Only in the midst of the questioning and temptation, the doubt and near-despair that daily experience brings with it, does the "sense" of the word of the cross become clear. Here, faith "lives in constant tension with its antithesis."[74] This is what *Anfechtung* meant for Luther: There is nothing detached, abstracted, "above-it-all" about true theology or about the truly Christian life.[75] It unfolds in the thick of human experience, in all its contradictions, difficulties, and negations. "Faith is only faith because it is exposed to the forces of temptation."[76]

Luther believed that a theology of glory contradicted human experience by promising what such a theology could never deliver: escape from real life, which is replete with evil, sin, death, and temptation. A theology of the cross, on the other hand, pointed to "a gospel that drove men into the world, not away from it; that opened their eyes to what was there, rather than assisting them to look past what was there."

> ... [W]hat makes Luther's theology a theology *of the cross* and not ... a theology of glory, is that the gospel is for him not the good news of *deliverance from* the experience of negation so much as it is the permission and command to enter into that experience with hope.[77]

Equip-ment[78]

The theology of the cross, finally, has implications for the way we live. "[T]he aim of the theology of the cross ... is a right use of reality."[79] Insofar as it orients the believer toward this aim, this "eminently practical"[80] theology functions to equip him or her in two dynamically and mutually interrelated ways: to live a life that is conformed to and participates in that of Christ, and to "call the thing what it actually is."

The attempt to explain how the theology of the cross equips the believer in these ways must begin by asserting

quite forcefully that "[f]or Luther, concern for the true knowledge of God and concern for the right ethical attitude [were]
not separate and distinct but ultimately one and the same."[81]
Luther's interest was not to propose a commendable ethical
program or a definitive interpretive framework, whose adop-
tion could ensure the rightly lived, or at least the rightly
perceived, life.[82] Scholastic theology was, after all, such a
framework, and the Roman church was, among other things,
the institutional form of such a framework. Luther's struggle
with scholastic theology and Roman church led to his breaking from the authoritarian faith they nurtured, a faith that
negated convictions forged in his daily experience and tem-
pered as he listened for the word God spoke into his life,
a word he found in—but never identified solely with—the
Bible. Luther's theology of the cross, which responded and
corresponded to his struggles of conscience, had the practical function of "lead[ing] a person out of his spectator
stance,"[83] of "bring[ing] the believer into a relationship, fraught
with tension, with the kingdom of the world."[84] In the first
instance, this referred to Luther himself. To be engaged fully
was for Luther a "right use of reality" that the cross not only
permitted but entailed. In this sense, the theology of the
cross was "a way of speaking about theology that
participate[d] in the same brokenness of life it [sought] to
describe."[85] By the same token, the speaker—a theologian
of the cross—was one who participated in the life such a
theology illuminated.

But how could such participation occur? In one sense,
it occurred as a life conformed to the cross of Christ. Luther's
contention that "God is known only in suffering" declared
two, or perhaps three, things. First, as we have seen, it
asserted that God's self-revelation occurs definitively on the
cross, in the suffering and death of Jesus. Second, it af-
firmed that only in the midst of his or her own suffering
could the believer come to know God. And third—and
perhaps most crucial for the "practical" function of his

theology—its apparent ambiguity actually pointed with great clarity and nuance to the profound correlation between the One who, in suffering, revealed to humans God's nature and intention for them, on the one hand, and those ones who, in their suffering, were enabled to know that nature and intention for them, on the other. This was for Luther true knowledge of God.

How this actually worked, Luther believed, was not at all clear to reason; it was simply not "reasonable" by the world's lights. But that it worked in the life of the believer, *simul iustus et peccator* all the while, was quite clear— certainly to Luther.

It is crucial that this dimension of the theology of the cross be understood to have emerged very directly out of Luther's life experience. This was a theology with a point of view—a particular, existentially grounded point of view. Any honorable attempt to describe the theology of the cross must underscore both the importance of this sort of obser- vation and the importance of the particular point of view— Luther's—that grounded his theology. No theology emanates from or heads into empty space; but in trying to make sense of the intimacy of the relationship Luther describes between the cross of Christ and the "cross" of the believer, it would be a great mistake to overlook the sense in which Luther spoke his theological mind in terms of his own daily expe- rience. There was nothing abstract, nothing divorced from daily life, in his theology.

"Man does not possess true knowledge as the result of an aptitude, but only as one 'who [in Luther's words] has been reduced to nothing through cross and suffering'."[86] This was talk from faith's conviction, not reason's specula- tion, which is in part why it is difficult to determine whether this sort of talk can be intelligible apart from faith. But the "logic" of the theology of the cross was neither linear nor deductive, and so it could not be presented as if it were. Luther's contention that one becomes a theologian (of the cross, presumably) not by speculating but by living and dying, was immediately and profoundly relevant. His theological standpoint expressed both his private terror of standing before a wrathful and righteous God draped in all his works-defined unworthiness, and the well-founded fears he faced because of professional, legal, and physical dangers that surrounded him as a public figure, "doing theology in the face of death," as von Loewenich suggests.[87]

It was not as if, given the course he was pursuing, he could have seen things from some other perspective above or beside the tensions his theology, polemics, and demeanor aroused and exacerbated. And, as he declared at the Diet at Worms, it was not as if he could have chosen some other course. The point is, perhaps, that he appears neither to have thought nor to have felt that a believer could be "safe" vis-à-vis the task of living or, more narrowly, that a theologian could be "over against" the task of theology. These tasks themselves drove one to the heart of human living and dying: precisely the only place where one could and would find the incarnate, crucified God, the same One (and the only One) who could and would equip one to fulfill these theological and existential tasks.

The "practicality" of the theology of the cross begins, then, with the sense in which it equips believers for participation in a life conformed to that life made possible through the living and dying of Jesus Christ. The theology of the cross does not "prescribe" such a life, as if one could choose it as one of several ethical options; in this sense it rejects both moralism, which "seeks the cross," and legalism, which requires conformity to the cross as a condition of justification. It simply illuminates what Luther saw as the necessary and dynamic mutuality of true knowledge of God and daily living—what Luther called a constant dying and rising with Christ[88]—in that knowledge.

It may be worth remarking on the difficulty, not to say foolishness, of attempting to describe the exact forms conformation to Christ take in the life of any particular believer. Like Luther, each believer will experience his or her own trials, or *Anfechtungen*, for all "are deeply involved participants in the [hand-to-hand] conflict between God and the devil. . . . " Whatever the manifestations of this conflict, however, Luther believed that

> [t]o be conformed to Christ means nothing else but experiencing the fact of the cross also in our lives. When the cross remains not simply a fact of history, but when it is erected in the midst of our lives, then we are people who have been conformed to Christ[89]

—a state of things that is itself a gift of God, not the result of our own efforts.

At its heart Luther's theology of the cross unapologetically describes a life (one might hazard to say, Luther's life) under the cross. A significant part of what preserves it from being simply his private theology and commends it to other believers is that Luther did not identify and claim his own (or any other individual's) experience as authoritative—he rarely wrote or spoke of it—nor did he hesitate at any moment to direct attention away from himself, toward the God whose self-revelation comprised the very possibility of justification and of theological talk about it.[90]

If there is anything frustrating about attempting to explicate the practical implications of Luther's theology of the cross, this frustration may stem from the predictable and sincere desire of the pragmatically minded to know, not what something implies for practice but rather what something is good for and how it works, and to be able to rationalize and regularize its application by means of rules and procedures that have foreseeable outcomes. There is, in other words, a keenly instrumental interest at work—an interest to which the theology of the cross does not respond; one could almost say that by its very nature it cannot.

Luther's description of the theologian of the cross as one who calls a thing by its right name suggests one way to understand how it is that the theology he explicates does not lend itself to an instrumentally defined usefulness. Like much else in Luther's theology, what he said here must be understood in the context of what he saw as the larger theological and ecclesiastical issues of his day, issues that have been already been explicated in this chapter. For present purposes, the significance of calling "the thing what it actually is" lies in the contrast Luther drew between those who do this, and those who "call . . . evil good and good evil"; who "prefer . . . works to suffering, glory to the cross, strength to weakness, wisdom to folly, and, in general, good to evil"; and who "love works and the glory of works."[91]

Luther's sharpest quarrel was with those whose capacities to make the most meaningful, fundamental distinctions and choices and to discern what was truly of value were confounded utterly by self- rather than cross-defined standards. Luther drew what one knows, or rather, what one does not know—"He who does not know Christ does not know God hidden in suffering"[92]—into a seamless relationship with what one does: "they hate the cross and suffering and love works and the glory of works."[93] One is not surprising in view of the other, nor the other in view of the one.

Theologians of glory—priests, popes, and academics—used power and position to misname, Luther argued; they benefited from an ecclesial and sacramental system that depended on calling good evil and evil good. These theologians of glory, oblivious to the gospel (as Luther read it), ignored the point of reference for the whole naming project: God would be found where God was least expected, where—

according to the world's lights—one would least want to be, oneself.

For Luther, theology's object was the relationship between God and human persons. Theology that lost sight of this relationship would always call God—and humankind—by the wrong names. "True theology and recognition of God," Luther wrote, "are in the crucified Christ."[94] The cross reverses and puts right the way in which humans come to know who God is and what that implies for their self-knowledge and their daily living, in that knowledge, *coram Deo*. In this sense, the cross becomes the epistemic fulcrum, the point on which true reality and the gift to see it, and name it, hinge. Luther's theology of the cross explicates this and in doing so equips the believer to call the thing by its right name.

A comment on faith.[95] How is the fundamental truth the theology of the cross describes—that God, beyond all comprehension, makes God's self known in opposition to all that human wisdom would call divine—to be grasped by human beings? Given the utter reversal of all self-defined human efforts to define or respond to reality that this truth requires, how *can* it make any sort of sense to humans themselves? How is it that the theology of the cross equips one to live?

The best—indeed, the only—response to all these questions is, "in faith." But this response, though truthful, does not explain itself, at least not theologically. Perhaps most critical to Luther's understanding of faith was his clarity about the fact that faith was not something willed or accomplished by humans. "Luther's concept of faith," writes Althaus,

> has nothing in common with any attempt to create strength and courage within ourselves by our own efforts, such as "positive thinking," nor is it related to a psychological condition of confidence

which can exist without an object of trust and apart from a personal relationship.[96]

That is to say, faith in Luther's sense is not a private, inner feeling; it is not something one has "in oneself" or in isolation. It is, rather, an act of God, God's gift. It is the human's response to the word of life, the word God speaks, without which there could be no response.

The nature of faith, Luther wrote, is "to see what one does not see, and not see, what one sees."[97] Oriented in faith, the theologian of the cross glimpses the self-revelation of God in the humiliated, crucified Nazarene carpenter. This human revelation of the hidden God is trusted to be the One who promises life and makes good on that promise. The notion of faith encompasses *what is believed*; it also describes *what is lived* in and because of one's believing. The empirical reality of this theologian's daily life, including its own experiences of trouble, suffering, and death, is the arena in which God's promise summons out faith and enables it as a disposition of trust realized in concrete acts. "Luther does not think of faith as existing in and of itself . . . . [He] does not imagine that any moment of life could be lived without faith or in neutrality toward faith. . . . "[98] Life is itself the exercise of faith.

In the theology of the cross, faith is the counterpart of the hiddenness of God (if God were visible, comprehensible, that would not be God, and faith would be irrelevant in any case). Articulated in the terms of the *theologia crucis*, faith involves an entrance into darkness: the casting away of all man-made notions of God, even of all man-made initiatives toward God. The cross confounds all human expectations, beginning with the most basic—existential—ones, and including the most ambitious—metaphysical—ones. Out of *these* depths, the human cries out for help to the God who cannot be seen. This is the beginning of faith, a forsaking of the illusion that one can save oneself, justify oneself, give oneself life.

Faith's abandonment of self-justification does not occur in a vacuum; it occurs in that faith hears and recognizes the word of the cross, a word of promise that is spoken directly and personally—*pro me*, Luther would say—into the heart.[99] "Justification is received *with* faith," Althaus writes, "that is, in the form of faith . . . . God justifies a man by giving him faith."[100]

The experience of everyday life teaches and continuously reminds one that indeed faith's object is a word of promise, not yet something fully realized. But in light of God's gift of faith, the experience of everyday life is itself also an experience of faith, faith as something real, neither ethereal nor abstract. Von Loewenich describes how this concept of faith affected Luther's life:

> . . . [M]atured by his battles for the gospel and enriched by experiences, [he] traded in [a] negatively defined concept of faith [as an entrance into darkness] for a positive one. . . . The quietistic elements of faith give way to the activistic, the world-shunning elements give way to those that shape the world.[101]

For Luther faith described and inscribed a life lived in recognition of the fact that one's life itself was not chosen but given, and that the point and purpose of one's life were framed within the relationship one has with the Giver. The Giver's loving intention and gracious will toward humans are revealed in human history and the present moment— chiefly in the cross and in the *Anfechtung* the Christian must face—in terms only faith could recognize. Neither what is revealed nor how the revelation occurs can skip over the human beings this revelation is meant for; but none of this is self-evident. It must all be played out in faith, in experience. Faith takes form within human experience because that is the medium within which God's initiative toward humankind occurs, in Christ and in the lives of individual Christians. Faith is both the starting point and the goal of experience.

One of Luther's most eloquent descriptions of faith appears in his Preface to the Epistle of St. Paul to the Romans:

> Faith is not the human notion and dream that some people call faith. . . . Faith . . . is a divine work in us which changes us and makes us altogether different . . . . [I]t is a living, busy, active, mighty thing, this faith . . . . Faith is a living, daring confidence in God's grace, so sure and certain that the believer would stake his life on it a thousand times.[102]

Such a "living, daring confidence in God's grace" is precisely what equips the theologian of the cross to live a life conformed to Christ's, and to call things by their right names.

Gathering Steam

In this chapter my chief concern has been to offer a sympathetic but fair account of Luther's theology of the cross in its emergence and in its functions—an account that could hold its own among theologians and yet inform those who, for reasons of unfamiliarity or skepticism, would not have imagined Luther to be a worthwhile conversation partner. I especially hope that I have persuaded or at least intrigued feminist skeptics, particularly those who may have read Chapter 1 with interest (or even enthusiasm) and then encountered this chapter with resistance.

Luther is a fascinating interlocutor. I would argue that both the style of his thought and the substance of his theology of the cross suggest warm "affinities" with the style and in some cases the substance of the critiques, insights, and challenges feminist epistemologists have offered. In what follows, readers may judge for themselves whether my contention holds water.

Drafting an Epistemology of the Cross

At this point, I must return for a moment to the Preface and to the experience it describes. The proposal I wish to make is an attempt to make useful conceptual sense of that experience, a kind of sense that may also find resonance with others, most of whom will not have had that particular experience, but may have had one like it in another context. Simply and briefly, what happened to me in El Salvador was that I discovered something I had not known before—which might be to say, something I had not known *in the particular way* I came to know it: in a way that drew me in, implicated me, required an account from me, compelled my response—and somehow enabled it.

In trying to describe this sort of coming-to-know experience, I am not interested in prescribing it. Even assuming that the process it depicts is something others have experienced or might recognize, it is not clear to me that such an experience can be prescribed. I would instead commend the description, which, while deeply rooted in the particularities of my own experience, is painted here with broader, somewhat abstract brushstrokes. The conceptual "story" reflects my conviction that what we come to know may lead us to seek or create a frame of reference that seems to help us make sense of our experiences. It seems clear, too, that this is itself an ongoing process, in which experiences and meaning-making symbols and frameworks inform and shape one another.[1]

The phenomena that comprise "what happened to me in El Salvador" move each day further into my past. Even as their immediacy as "event/s" fades, however, their vividness as points of reference persists. My concern to give an account of "what I have seen and heard" grows out of my experience of its ongoing capacity to illuminate: As both historic event and metaphor, it has helped me "make meaning" in my life and my thinking (including my theology), and I believe it will continue to do so. That I wish to render it useful to others, too, clearly suggests that I do not believe that what happened is a closed book, either in the sense of being only my private personal experience or in the sense of being just a good story with an already established ending.

There are no doubt other serviceable versions of the same story, some of which might be more, and some less, easily integrated into an epistemological proposal that is based in Luther's theology of the cross and informed by feminist perspectives. The point is, I am offering this draft proposal, not simply because I think it is a good idea, but because the experience I had then compelled me, and continues to compel me, to try to make sense of it—in terms of its occurrence (now in my past) as well as in terms of its ongoing claims on my living. As it happens, the variety of resources I have found useful in preparing this essay suggest that my own experience, necessarily particular, also has a place within a much larger mosaic. That the patterns of that mosaic demonstrate affinities rather than identities convinces me that my particular contribution is as important to the realization of the whole as it is necessary for my self-realization.

Clarifying Terms

This chapter is intended to take some of the first, provisional steps toward what I will call an "epistemology of the cross." It is an approach aimed to help focus our late-twentieth-century, North American attention, particularly as Christians, on what should govern our knowing and where we must look to learn it as we seek to live morally responsible lives. That the term "epistemology" eludes a precise definition does not discourage me from using it. Discussions of what it refers to, what it means, and what questions it awakens have been productive. As long as discussants are willing to explain what they mean by "epistemology" or "epistemological," others can criticize, correct, or subscribe, and the conversation is likely to spark further insights about knowing, knowers, and knowledge.

In calling what I propose an "epistemology *of the cross*," I am alluding directly to Luther's theology of the cross. I do so in the belief that Luther's theology of the cross can be understood legitimately in terms of epistemological dimensions and promise. Implicit (and sometimes explicit) among Luther's concerns, I would argue, were questions about who knowers are, what they/we know, where they/we seek knowledge, and what we/they use it for. All the same, it must be abundantly clear that this draft/proposal for an "epistemology of the cross" is mine, not Luther's. I would be delighted if I could persuade Luther to "join up" in realizing this program. But I am not interested in proving that Luther would have done what I am trying to do; rather, I am interested in showing how certain of Luther's key notions are quite serviceable in orienting, shaping, limiting, or justifying a project that I believe would have value independently of Luther and his theology.

In this spirit, too, what follows is not intended as a complete alternative epistemology, nor as a comprehensive program for a theory of knowledge. Built on a recognition that all knowledge is constructed, serves purposes, values particular sources, and so forth, it attempts to respond to questions like these: What sort of epistemological terms of reference does the theology of the cross suggest? To the extent that, say, as Christians, we can choose the epistemological "lens" through which we peer, what sort of "prescription" will enable us to see what we need to see? Can the theology of the cross help us epistemologically, that is, in terms of the sources, locales, sorts of knowing we should value as we seek to live faithfully?

This is also an invitation to others to collaborate in, and to elaborate, this "work in progress." If it is to be of use, it must continue to be exercised, criticized, tried out and tried on for size. In order to foment discussion of an issue I consider pressing, I have brought together and spoken (identifiably and evenhandedly, I hope) for some unlikely conversation partners. If the ball that begins to roll here is rolling in the right direction, I hope it will gather momentum; if it ought not to roll further, I hope the provocation offered here will incite some attempts to stop it. In either case, I will consider this effort to have been worthwhile.

Bringing in Luther

At the heart of Luther's theology of the cross is what I would call a profoundly epistemological question: the question about knowledge of God. Among many scholars, von Loewenich highlights this insight. For Luther, he writes, "knowledge of God comes into being at the cross of Christ."[2] The tight corollary is that the proper subject of theology is the divine-human relationship; that is, the only fruitful—indeed, the only possible—theological reflection occurs in the light of what transpires between God and humans, between humans and God.[3] Without revelation—the "stuff"

98

that without God's gifting activity would never be known to humans—there is, of course, no reflection at all worthy of the name "theology." But it is crucial to appreciate the utter centrality of God's epistemological "friendliness" to humans that is expressed in Luther's insistence on the divine-human relationship as the locus of all "proper" theology.[4]

At no moment—least of all in Luther's work—should one mistake theology for faith. Knowledge of God does not and never has come through theology![5] (Although theologians certainly teach this, they tend to have a harder time than most remembering it.) At this juncture it is more important to post this warning sign than to enter into an in-depth discussion of the distinction. Luther excoriated the scholastic theologians of his day in large measure because the knowledge they generated fueled the illusion, which Luther considered spiritually pernicious, that God could be "known" theologically—and that any God who could be known could certainly be bargained with.

Salvation is not an epistemological question: not generally, and certainly not for Luther. Human salvation, or justification, or coming to faith/utter trust in God, does not depend on what a person knows theologically—or nontheologically. Moreover, lived experience continuously made it clear to Luther that even good theology was an imperfect, stumbling, and sometimes internally contradictory—but above all, hu-man—attempt to describe, clarify, and interpret what God revealed to/through faith *in the daily living of it*. What "made" theologians was their daily, creaturely living, not their intense study of the "things of God" as theology or the church defined them. According to Luther, "Theological knowledge is won by experiencing it."[6] Theology was existential.

Faith, too, is existential: It is not "laid on" over the dailiness of life, but rather pervades it, even makes the living of life possible. In this sense, the "knowledge of God" born of and borne by faith is for Luther intimately related to knowledge of the world—call it "ordinary knowledge"—

and theology that tries to describe faith's knowledge of God is also intimately related to all other kinds of knowing: of things, persons, or what we might call "truths." I would argue that for Luther these realms of knowledge are related in several ways and for several reasons.

In one sense, "knowledge of God" and "ordinary knowledge" (including theological knowledge)—I ask indulgence for the use of these clumsy concepts, distinguished here mainly to argue their relatedness—are related because, from the perspective of Luther's theology, they set each other off: They help to define one another, to some degree, by spelling out what each is *not*, at least as much as they do by spelling out what each *is* or deals with. They also make each other possible, in the sense that each has its proper bailiwick. In other words, faith's knowledge of God both "frames" other knowledge and "frees" the justified sinner/knower to know all kinds of "ordinary" things. Finally, because it functions in these two ways, it also requires and enables epistemological accountability: Human knowers must and can act responsibly in the world, in relation to others.

Once we know, with Luther, what we cannot and do not know—for example, God, directly; anything that contributes to our own justification or salvation—then what must we know to live our lives as faithful people? The answer to this question is not defined by its content. Rather, the answer to this question is a series of other questions that have to do with the sources and purposes of our knowledge. These are epistemological questions, questions less of fact or even interpretation than of method. They are questions to which I believe an epistemology of the cross can help us supply answers. In fact, what we need to know as faithful people, we cannot know without an epistemology of the cross.

Insofar as what follows draws on Luther's theology of the cross, then, its focus is most certainly not on answering the question, How do we come to know God? Or even, How does the theology of the cross help us to describe what we come to know about God? It is rather more complicated, perhaps: What *epistemological* implications can we draw from how the *theology* of the cross seeks to interpret our lives? For the most part, the response to this question will be drawing away from mainly theological discourse—intentionally. Whatever discomfort this approach may induce among those used to talking about the theology of the cross theologically will, I trust, not last long.

Kinds of Knowing

There may also be considerable anticipatory discomfort, however, among those who are suspicious—often, justifiably—when Christian theologians begin to talk as if they have something, after all, to teach those who left the fold, or those who never wanted any part of it. Douglas John Hall, a theologian who is deeply sympathetic to the distances such suspicion creates and maintains, admonishes co-Christians that

> the claims of Christian faith can be entertained seriously only if they are accompanied by strong evidence that their advocates have opened themselves existentially to the rigors of the epistemological question.[7]

In the interest of staking out what could be called common epistemological ground with those who do not describe themselves as Christians, Hall provides a threefold typology of knowing that distinguishes *knowledge, acknowledgment,* and *trust.* Doing so, he also clarifies his judgment that the epistemological "offense" of Christian faith resides in the quality—"that is to say, with the nature of what is known, and the mode of knowing it"[8]—rather than the quantity of what Christians claim to know. Hall distinguishes these three types of knowing:

1. The first, _knowledge_, is essentially the possession of information. Christianity is an historical faith, Hall argues, based upon events, and the events to which it refers itself must be passed along by teaching and learning this information. Unless "just the facts" are known, faith has no "stuff." But "the facts," while chronologically prior in the life of a person, are not themselves sufficient.

2. The second, _acknowledgment_, involves the transformation of what is "simply" known into what is significant, or relevant in a special way. This is an unpredictable—and sometimes apparently arbitrary—occurrence; the word "mysterious" may also describe it. What becomes acknowledgment for one person may, under the same circumstances, remain just plain information for another. "Something happened," one is heard to say of this change; "I can't explain it, but I see things differently now."

3. The third, _trust_, implies a state of belief, or commitment—a "depth of relationship," Hall says:

   Sacrament.

...I find myself deciding—that this other one has some kind of claim on me and, correspondingly, that I have some kind of responsibility for this other.[9]

An interpretation of these three types of knowing (and particularly the third type) specifically in terms of Christian faith is possible only in the context of what Christians call

102

"revelation," which is not propositional, but rather the dis- *def of revel.* closure of a presence: God's. The key difference between knowing oriented toward and enlivened by this divine self-revelation, and knowing that is not so oriented and enlivened, is a difference in perspective rather than in content. (Some of the difficulties involved in sorting out the imprint of this perspective, particularly as shaped by the theology of the cross, show up in this chapter.)

Neither Christians nor skeptics need abandon the possibility of a common epistemological agenda. Hall argues convincingly that

> "knowing" in . . . Christian theology is . . . continuous with knowing in human experience and language generally . . . . [It] is not of another order, as if in the Christian the ordinary faculties . . . of "the thinking animal" had been replaced by something else! . . . God does not circumvent the human in God's self-communication.[10]

Whatever we come to know, we come to know under conditions of time and space; this is true whether what we come to know is God, a proposition, or another person.

What is most important about Hall's typology, it seems to me, is that it does much to help set up the conditions for a productive conversation about epistemology across battlefield lines that historically have been drawn quite sharply: on the one hand, by Christian theologians who have fused, or confused, what Hall distinguishes as "knowledge" and "trust," and, on the other, by secular thinkers (feminists among them) who dismiss across the board what Christians "know" (or think they know) because it appears to be rooted in a reality not unlike the Twilight Zone, to have to be taken "on faith"—an expression whose epistemological meaning neither Christian nor secular knowers seem to understand fully. To make the distinctions Hall makes is to recognize at the very least that Christians' knowing and others' knowing can be talked about using the same language. It is hard to see what sort of objections secular feminists would raise to such distinctions even outside the context of Christian theology.

It also seems clear on the face of it that a more nuanced understanding of knowing in Christian faith and theology opens doors to what might be mutually edifying conversation with secular feminist thinkers whose critiques of traditional epistemology were treated in Chapter 1. Some of these critiques focus on how traditional epistemology defines legitimate knowledge. They observe, among other things, an unsurprising, frequent correlation between an understanding of knowledge as "scientifically objective" and an understanding of science as the universal, transhistorical effort of man [sic] to tell the "one true story" about reality or nature; or a persistent attempt to correlate the sturdiness of propositional knowledge, on the one hand, with the establishment of moral tranquillity as the successful resolution of a series of correct propositions derived from observations about how people/objects behave and from principles about how "things" should work, on the other. In either case, feminists' critiques call attention to both how shamelessly power legitimates the knowing that suits it, and how out of touch knowing so legitimated can be with what else there is to know. Some Christian theologians would subscribe heartily to these insights; others could learn something.

Among feminists working in the area of epistemology, Lorraine Code, Elizabeth Kamarck Minnich, and Evelyn Fox Keller (each of whose work mentions others who have been working on the same problem) have suggested alternative approaches that require relinquishing narrow and rigid definitions of knowing. Code's wry discussion of the implications of "knowing other people" for reconceiving how we define knowledge, including scientific knowledge, is illustrative:

104

> ... [I]t is surely no more preposterous to argue that people should try to know physical objects in the nuanced way that they know their friends than it is to argue that they should try to know people in the unsubtle way that they claim to know physical objects.[11]

The purpose of the foregoing is not to establish an exact fit between the sort of theologically oriented epistemological typology Hall proposes, on the one hand, and the secular feminist critiques that have played such a part in producing what Hall calls "worldly reason's new modesty,"[12] on the other. It is rather to bolster with further evidence the suggestion that Luther's theology and the work of secular feminists may be drawn together in useful—and unapologetic—conversation about knowing.

An Epistemology of the Cross

According to one useful understanding of epistemology, it provides a "frame of reference" for adjudicating questions about the conditions, legitimacy, and adequacy of knowers, knowing, and knowledge. It may be that the *theology* of the cross is itself just such a thing. Most treatments of it, however, tend to insist that the person who wants to engage the theology of the cross—for whatever purposes—must comprehend it on its own, theological terms. Once acceded to, however, this approach may make it quite difficult to see where *else* one might go with what one has learned in the theological arena. So, as I say, while the theology of the cross may itself be an epistemology, it might be more prudent to refer to it as background for what I am calling here an epistemology of the cross. It acts as a kind of continuo, which, while it does not demand attention, keeps the musical train on the tracks.

In a theological conversation, I have suggested, Luther's *theologia crucis* functions as critique, announcement, and equip-ment; another way of putting this would be to say that it functions critically, constructively, and ethically. To use these terms is not to assert that what Luther's theology does or how it does it can be divided into neat, noninteractive packages. Quite the contrary is true: none of these dimensions does much of anything without the others, nor does what any of them does have much significance without the others. As with so much of Luther, for the sake of "coming to terms with" and "being able to make use of," things may be distinguished that really cannot be separated.

I would like now to move along from the strictly theological conversation about the theology of the cross into a conversation more plainly concerned with knowing: knowing about things, people, situations, that insist on or ought to require our engagement as we live our everyday lives. I assay this partly for reasons expressed in the early pages of this book: because of a sense of accountability to and for my religious and theological heritage, which I believe has continuing ethical as well as theological usefulness. But I do so also because, with Hall and others, I believe that our coming to know, regardless of what or who it is that we come to know, occurs through the same marvelous apparatus. We need not—I would say, we dare not—set aside some part of ourselves as we deconstruct, examine, reconstruct, adopt, or set aside our learnings. The profound and mysterious matter of what we Christians believe revelation reveals refuses to be set aside; but among the things we also believe is that there is a vast difference between our talk about what revelation reveals and revelation itself. The ensuing proposal is predicated on the confidence that we can "talk epistemology" well without disguising our theology, and that both our epistemology and our theology may benefit as a result.

To whom is this epistemological project directed? As I indicated in the Preface, I believe my task is

> not to theologize for the marginalized, but rather for ones like me: white, relatively privileged North American Christians who want to know "what time it is" and, in the face of that reality, how we can live most faithfully.

I take quite seriously the co-responsibility I bear for causing and tolerating the oppressive consequences of systems and ideologies from which I benefit much more, and much more often, than I suffer. Such systems and ideologies thrive on racism, sexism, heterosexism, and gross maldistribution of economic resources and political power within nations and across international boundaries in all directions. I also take quite seriously the ways in which the religious tradition I am part of has fomented, exacerbated, and then walked past much of the suffering caused by people and institutions that have claimed to be God's very messengers.

I do not plead innocence.

And yet the cause of liberation deserves, and needs, more than a guilty plea by those conscious of their relative privilege. It is better served, it seems to me, by the sort of *metanoia*, or turning around, that involves—*in addition to and as part of* an acceptance of responsibility for causing and benefiting from the oppression of others—rigorous self-examination leading to course-corrections. Because of the ways in which I am woven into and caught up in collectivities whose reach is far broader than my own, this is a process that requires collaboration from "others like me"— whether these are professionals, women, whites, Christians, North Americans, theologians, or any combination of these or other groupings. In order for the needed collaboration to occur, I have a responsibility to carry the matter into the midst of those who should be so engaged. Certainly this is not the end of my responsibility to act, but it is just as certainly an essential part of that responsibility.[13]

Both this chapter and the next will explore some of the complications arising from what I believe is a generalizable lack of "innocence," which can be understood productively in various ways. Let me be very clear on this point: To say that no one is innocent is not to let everyone, or anyone, off the ethical hook; nor is it to invite a comparison of degrees of responsibility for or subjectedness to oppression. It is simply to grant that, given our multiple and sometimes contradictory, non-innocent "identities," the matter of discerning and setting ethical priorities becomes quite complicated.

With this proposal, I wish to carry the conversation about a contemporary theology of the cross[14]—clearly rooted in, but not the same as Luther's sixteenth-century version— into the hall where secular feminists, among other concerned collectivities, have gathered to shake up and sort out and stitch together terms of reference that serve all of us by

> . . . offer[ing] a more adequate, richer, better account of the world, in order to live in it well and in critical, reflexive relation to our own as well as others' practices of domination and the unequal parts of privilege and oppression that make up all positions.[15]

In preparation for this conversation, I believe that theologians who have claimed Luther's theology of the cross as intellectual or spiritual private property could benefit greatly from seeing it instead (as I do) as a more widely useful intellectual and spiritual resource, a part of the human commons. In that role, it is of course as subject to healthy criticism as it is available for constructive purposes. In any case, as I argued in the last chapter, the "right use of reality" suggested in the above citation is just the sort of project the *theologia crucis* is good for.

The material that follows (a) proposes elements of an epistemology of the cross; and (b) explains how an epistemology of the cross constituted by such elements works.

Some Elements of an Epistemology of the Cross

In real life it is impossible to separate entirely the elements that comprise an epistemology of the cross from how it works. However, in order to look as carefully as possible at the proposed framework, this section will make the distinction and treat them sequentially. In the process, most of what is needed can be drawn from Chapter 1, which sought to describe the concerns and critiques of feminist epistemologies without referring explicitly to Luther; and Chapter 2, which aimed to lay out Luther's theology of the cross without particular reference to feminist issues. This is the place, then, where I will bring them together, creating a sturdier alloy where possible, leaving them next to one another where that seems prudent. The point of the exercise is not only the discussion it provokes—a worthy if partial goal—but more important, the usefulness of an epistemological proposal that is indebted to both conversation partners but captive to neither.

A series of questions will help sort out some of the elements that I believe comprise the emerging epistemological approach:

1. What does this approach say about power?[16]
2. What does it say about experience?
3. What does it say about objectivity?
4. What role does accountability play?

Considerations of power, experience, objectivity, and accountability are both central to any epistemology worth its salt and indicative of its bearings. Responses to each of these questions will suggest the sort of "disposition" one

would expect an epistemology of the cross to foster and/
or reflect.

Power. The term "power" casts a wide net, gathering in a
multiplicity of relevant meanings and associations. To examine what an epistemology of the cross has to say about
power is principally to underscore the *critical* element at
its center.

Power in epistemological garb, as feminist critiques
have pointed out, affords itself many of the same luxuries
it indulges in elsewhere: insulated by the wealth of possibilities the privilege of power confers, power-epistemology
allows itself to ignore limits and resolve ambiguities, including those that doubt generates or accompanies. When limits
and ambiguity are experienced, the framework of a doubtless "epistemologia gloriae" (epistemology of glory) reads
them as humiliations rather than as features of the daily
human landscape that should require of us creatures only
sobriety, not courage, to acknowledge.

An epistemology of glory has all the answers, or thinks
it can get them—if not now, then eventually. If necessary,
it takes the liberty of re-framing the most difficult questions
themselves in more manageable terms. The neat partnership
between epistemological hubris and the quasi-religious belief in progress is as pernicious in determining to banish
even the thought of human limits as it is effective in invent-
ing political and economic projects to institutionalize itself.
There is a kind of "never-look-back," "don't-look-down"
single-mindedness at work here; reality is what subscribers
to this epistemology of power say it is.

An epistemology of the cross will not ignore, dismiss,
or underestimate the positive epistemological infrastructure
(of knowers, knowledge-generating projects, and "items" of
knowledge) necessary to sustain "one-true-story" science,
philosophy, or religion. Rather, it will *engage* it critically. An
epistemology of the cross will harbor an intrinsic suspicion

of power, imaged and experienced in its most common format—domination, or power-over. This suspicion continuously questions the legitimacy of the powerful as knowers and their right to add to or subtract from their ranks, by individual or by group; it also casts its beam on how knowledge is produced under conditions shaped and maintained by power-over. Finally, it scrutinizes whose interests and what causes are served, and what happens to designated "non-knowers," when knowledge is generated and used under the power-differentiated circumstances that usually obtain in real life. When Sandra Harding cites with approval "a feminist postmodernist suspicion of the relationship between accepted definitions of 'reality' and socially legitimated power," she could also be describing the stance suggested by an epistemology of the cross.[17]

An epistemology of the cross does not issue its critique of power-knowers or their knowledge claims from a neutral space—say, somewhere to the left of right and to the right of left. It identifies itself as an epistemological alternative, holding forth "over against" positive, power-defined knowledge; it challenges power defined as domination-over, refusing to be caught up in the terms such power dictates. In critiquing the epistemology of glory, an epistemology of the cross issues from a perspective learned with and from those—or those parts of one's own multiply identified self—relegated to the margins or backwoods of the "dominant meaning system" (Minnich). In contrast to the transcendent, global claims power-defined epistemologies make—claims rooted as much in a fear of real, creaturely limits as in an addiction to mastery of the surround—an epistemology oriented to the cross insists on the partialness of what can be known by any of us knowers, and/or by all of us together.[18] It lives, often uncomfortably, with ambiguity and doubt.

Power as it is being discussed here is played out in "politics"—in individual relationships, institutionally, in formally defined polities, internationally. Politics is both context and content for disputes about what constitutes legitimate knowledge, who may claim it, and what it is for. "What kind of politics," Haraway asks, "could embrace partial, contradictory, permanently unclosed constructions of personal and collective selves and still be faithful, effective . . . ?"[19] Among other things, how do power and an understanding of power shape epistemological frameworks and the justifying or resisting responses for which such frameworks may equip our constructed, "personal and collective selves"? One option able to inform the "kind of politics" Haraway writes of is an epistemology of the cross.

It may be fair to say that if an epistemology of the cross were about no other task, its contribution to the critique of power-as-domination would be sufficient.

Experience. For an epistemology of the cross, lived experience is the locale and the medium of all knowing.[20] This means a number of things, among them these:

(1) Knowing about people, propositions, even God, occurs in, with, and under the material realities of knowers' everyday lives. There certainly are other ways of apprehending or speaking about the existential realities within which, say, knowers come to know, but their concreteness, incarnateness, embodied-ness—all terms that point to the materiality of human experience—must never be lost from sight, as tends to happen when "experience" appears as a concept in traditional epistemological discourse.

Among the most eloquent expressions of the significance of embodiment to knowing, and one thoroughly compatible with an epistemology of the cross, can be found in Chung Hyun Kyung's *Struggle to Be the Sun Again.* The Korean feminist theologian writes of an "epistemology of the broken body," a framework for knowing inscribed, through storytelling, by Asian women's experience of suffering:

The power of storytelling lies in its *embodied truth*. Women talked about their concrete, historical life experience and not about abstract, metaphysical concepts. Women's truth was generated by their *epistemology of the broken body*. Women's bodies are the most sensitive receiver for historical reality. Their bodies record what has happened in their lives. Their bodies remember what it is like to be *no-body* and what it is like to be a *some-body*.[21]

It is also clear that the material realities of lived experience affect how knowing occurs—just as knowing affects what knowers do in, with, and about these realities.

(2) In emphasizing that lived experience is what "grounds" knowing, an epistemology of the cross also emphasizes the "given-ness" of the creaturely life that experience articulates. To recognize this "given-ness" does not mean not to accept the particular political or economic status quo (as if it reflected presumed orders of nature); it is rather to acknowledge that limits, in knowing as in other dimensions, accompany our (common) existence as human beings. This insight differentiates itself from a similar one in secular feminist discussion mainly in its distinctly theological basis.

(3) Partly in view of the critical disposition of an epistemology of the cross toward power- or privilege-based knowers and knowing, and partly because of its acknowledgment of creaturely limits, such an epistemology recognizes that experience is always interpreted, and that any interpretation is likely to be partial and contested.

For example, knowing based solely on what might be called "experiential foundationalism," or simply "having had X experience," can be problematic. Harding observes that while we

113

preserve the integrity and wisdom inherent in . . .
specific experiences, especially in previously ignored and devalued ones, [we must also come] to
terms with the fact that experience in many respects hides the realities of our lives: experience
"lies."[22]

There are no ironclad guarantees that unreflected experiences, whether from the center or from the margins, will
yield up insights that serve liberatory aims. The experience
of marginalization does not guarantee, by itself, the overcoming of cultural stereotypes—racist, classist, sexist, or
heterosexist—that some may associate more commonly with
the privileged. Like the ubiquity of multiple, sometimes
contradictory identities, loyalties, and interests within one
person, and within collectivities of persons who also have
some overarching commonalities, the traps of unprocessed,
"spontaneous consciousness" require that the epistemological authority of lived experience be subscribed to carefully,
as well as constantly.

(4) Experiences are lived by particular knowers and in
that sense have a "tailor-made" quality that, according to an
epistemology of the cross, invites attentiveness and resists
generalization. It is difficult to "collect" experiences into any
sort of category that can be said to be true of everyone's
living—except in a way that loses both its explanatory power,
as it departs or fades away from each one's living, and its
moral value, in accounting for *that* valuable person, and
that one, and *that* one.

(5) At the same time, an epistemology of the cross
grants prima facie value to the sort of knowing that comes
from the lived experience of struggle at the margins: these
are "limit-experiences," places that usually test the integrity
and purpose of knowers, and the durability and responsiveness of their knowing. Luther interpreted his many personal
experiences of suffering in terms as existential as they were

114

theological. He called them evidence of God's "alien work," which brought Luther the human being to his limits; he believed that only there, having experienced those limits, could he be convinced to throw himself into the arms of the One he otherwise refused. Only then, he believed, could and did he experience God's "proper work": the grace that *was* life and made his experience of every day possible. This could happen, Luther said, because of the realized mystery of sinners' participation in the cross of Jesus Christ, which was itself the participation of the self-revealing God in the cross of human brokenness: the "state of the art" of human existence. Hall's explanation makes Luther's interpretation more accessible:

> The cross belongs first to us—to [humankind, to everyone]. It becomes the cross of Jesus the Christ because only so can he identify with us and so break the power of what destroys us. The cross is the logical, "necessary" point to which the incarnation moves . . . because that is *our* destiny. . . . The theology of the incarnation is and remains a theology of the cross, for it proclaims a God whose will is to be with us. . . .[23]

What is the epistemological point? Knowing that ignores or papers over our individual and corporate human experiences of the cross is of little value and even less use in a world that testifies daily to the reality of such experiences. Even to cover "just the facts," any epistemology would have to account for these experiences. An epistemology of the cross takes them as its "permanent standing ground . . . [and the cross as] a symbol of the reality in which [we] participate . . . and into which [we] must again and again be initiated."[24] For an epistemology of the cross, then, to know truly on the basis of lived experience is to know from the margins: of life, of sanity, of dignity, of power. Coming to know in this way is possible because and by means of the incarnated mystery of solidarity.

This dimension of an epistemology of the cross shares with feminists a conviction that special value—both what might loosely be called "scientific" and what is surely "ethical"—attaches to knowing that emerges from those personal and collective quarters where resistance to injustice and suffering begins with the "knowing" of them. Here we may gain "perspective from those points of view which . . . promise . . . knowledge potent for constructing worlds less organized by axes of domination."[25]

Objectivity. Traditional science's epistemological approach prizes a metaphorical "Archimedean point" as the place from which one achieves "objectivity," that perspective from which (it seems to those who prize it) what one sees ("perception") and what is there ("reality") coincide. Because this point exists, science declares, objectivity can be "had"; it is, in a real sense, the exercise of control (at least the kind of control measurement and prediction promise). Once possessed, those who "have" objectivity are displaced only with great difficulty.

Feminist epistemologists claim, in contrast, that the mythical Archimedean point is located where prevailing cultural (including political) winds set it down, and that objectivity is a problematic, context-dependent notion.

An epistemology of the cross, while its critical disposition allows it to share the feminists' skepticism about traditional science's "objectivity," has a distinctive epistemological starting point: the foot of the cross. To stand there is not to claim or even to seek the objectivity positive science treasures; nor is it to content itself with the necessary relativization of objectivity as science has defined it. Instead, an epistemology of the cross seeks "to be *with* the victims . . . [where it becomes possible to come to know] . . . that it is not the

poor who are a problem to the rich, but the rich who are
a problem to the poor.[26] "To come to know" in this way,
in this sense, is to experience what liberation theologians
call an "epistemological break."[27] By means of a process or
an event (it is difficult to define it precisely), one who could
by all odds claim epistemological privilege becomes aware
of a complete reversal of the notion of "privilege," finds that
an extraordinary kind of truthfulness (not "objectivity") attaches to the "partial" perspective glimpsed from the vantage of the struggle of the poor, the discriminated-against,
the forgotten-about, the thrown-away.[28] It is "partial" both in
its frank partisanship and in its equally frank lack of concern about the "larger picture" whose purported completeness requires including the perspective of the rich, the
discriminator, the forgetter, the one who throws away.[29]

Jon Sobrino describes this phenomenon, which he
himself has undoubtedly experienced many times and which
he has witnessed as countless European and North American visitors have passed through his San Salvador parish.
From personal experience I can testify to the uncanny ac-
curacy of his words, quoted here at length:

> From the poor [we] receive, in a way hardly ex-
> pected, new eyes for seeing the ultimate truth of
> things and new energies for exploring unknown
> and dangerous paths. For [us] the poor are "oth-
> ers," and when [we] take on solidarity with them
> [we] undergo the experience of being sent to others
> only to find their own truth. At the very moment
> of giving [we] find [ourselves] expressing gratitude
> for something new and better that [we] have been
> given . . . . [W]hether this gratuitousness is explic-
> itly referred back to God or remains unidentified,
> it is clear that in aiding the poor one receives
> back from them meaning for one's life.[30]

As a result of such an "epistemological break," the power of objectivity, and the "objectivity" of the powerful, must be judged according to new and more stringent standards.

Whether the subjugated have a epistemological prior claim on "truth" is no more at issue than whether they are closer to God or spiritually more developed than those who are not subjugated. But an epistemology of the cross shares with feminist epistemologies the conviction that, to the degree that relatively undistorted and ethically defensible knowing matter, the place of the least favored—at the foot of the cross, in all its contemporary forms—is a better place to start than any place of domination could be. To be there is to be with those who "raise the deepest questions about what it really means to be human."[31] There is much that simply cannot be seen or known—about how things really are, and about ourselves in relation to that reality—without *being there.*

And yet there are significant difficulties in our getting to that epistemological "there." Referring to the lives of those "whose voices have led us to see the need to rethink our views of ourselves," Harding cautions, "It is crucial to avoid imagining that men and people of European descent in the dominant groups really do lead marginal lives. . . . We have not *had* [the] experiences [of the marginalized] and do not live their lives."[32] bell hooks, one of those who has led many white, professional, middle-strata feminist women to rethink our views of ourselves, observes this problematic keenly. "Often," she writes, "this speech about the 'Other' annihilates, erases:

> [You say,] 'No need to hear your voice when I can talk about you better than you can speak about yourself . . . . Only tell me about your pain[,] . . . your story. And then I will tell it back to you in a new way[,] . . . in such a way that it has become . . . my own. Re-writing you, I write myself

118

anew. I am still author, authority . . . and you are
now at the center of my talk.' Stop. We greet you
as liberators. '[W]e' . . . inhabit marginal space that
is not a site of domination but a place of resistance. Enter that space."[33]

hooks' words are bracing—and necessary—among those
feminists who are used to speaking and among those who
refuse to be silenced, those who are used to speaking *about*
and those who insist on being spoken *to* and *with*. "Enter
that space," she writes. "Let us meet there. Enter that space.
We greet you as liberators."[34] Her words unmask and reveal.
They also invite—cautiously, and with some hope.

Harding believes that relatively privileged people can
"choose to *become* 'marginalized,' " and in so doing, can
gain a more critical, clearer view of themselves as knowers
and doers—as people who are deeply implicated in the fact
of others' marginalization and deeply responsible to collaborate in the transformation that requires. " . . . [W]e can
learn," she writes, "to think and act *not* out of the 'spontaneous consciousness' of the social locations that history
has bestowed on us but out of the traitorous ones we
choose. . . ."[35]

What Harding calls "reinventing ourselves as 'other' "[36]
depends on the possibility that "we" (which must always be
specified) may be capable of embracing, within our multiply identified individual selves and among ourselves as groups
of selves, the "other/s," or marginalized one/s. These are
the subjects/knowers whose epistemological standpoints are
salutary almost in direct relation to their capacity to subvert
dominant knowledge projects; they/we are what make
it possible to speak of "strong objectivity" and liberatory
epistemologies in more than theoretical terms. This is all
very volatile, very delicate, and very important stuff.

An epistemology of the cross can offer some theologically informed support for the sort of project feminists like

Harding propose. To begin with this epistemology cannot be used by knowers whose claims to objectivity are predicated on domination, we have already indicated it harbors a deep suspicion of power-based knowledge claims and those who make them. This cross-based epistemology surprises us, drawing our attention and concern toward unexpected places and moments of coming to know: generally, those in which what Hall calls "the experience of negation" occurs—

> [i]n human suffering and degradation, in poverty and hunger, among the two thirds who starve, in races that are brought low, in exposure to the icy winds of the nihil, in the midst of hell. . . .[37]

We may discover such places as we look in the mirror at our individual, stitched-together selves: the physically healthy lesbian woman; the undocumented Salvadoran man; the well-paid health care professional disabled by AIDS; the African-American general; the white welfare mother. We may discover them in our ambivalences about the "categories" of persons with which we want to or others insist that we associate ourselves: those with whom we share, happily or unhappily, race, nation, religion, gender, sexual orientation, class, and so forth. We may also discover places of pain, difficulty, confusion, suffering, in the interstices among these individual and corporate identities, which is where we often come to existential terms with dilemmas that seem to pit us against ourselves and one another. An epistemology of the cross reminds us, too, that in the interest of "calling the thing what it is" we are well advised to remain sensitive to Minnich's cautionary words:

> Insofar as we speak and think and act in ways that make sense to other people within the domi-

nant meaning system, we cannot avoid participating . . . in precisely that which we wish to change.[38]

It is difficult to avoid such participation altogether. There is
no "innocent" place, epistemologically or otherwise.

Is there, then, a strategy that an epistemology of the
cross could subscribe to? Haraway's suggestion for the course
women's studies might follow seems quite compatible with
the approach an epistemology of the cross might favor:

> [We] must negotiate the very fine line between
> appropriation of another's (never innocent) expe-
> rience and the delicate construction of the just-
> barely-possible affinities, the just-barely-possible
> connections that might actually make a difference
> in local and global histories. . . . [39]

The emphasis here is on the negotiation of bare possibilities
for the sake of "connections that might make a difference."
Power-brokered objectivity has no role; humility and risk-
taking do. And none of it can be done without hope; one
might even call it hope against hope.

So: Is there any point to discussing objectivity in the
context of an epistemology of the cross? If objectivity is
defined as what gives the "one true story" of science, or
theology, epistemological pride of place, the answer is No.
It is a truism, not often honored in science or theology, that
there is always more than one version of any story. While
the speaker with the most expensive sound truck may have
something worthwhile to say, one must always consider the
source.

An epistemology of the cross would be more comfortable with Harding's notion of "strong objectivity," whose
peculiar strength rests on the participation of many knowers,
and among them, begins with the least favored, and a

121

commitment to critical examination of the causes of beliefs, especially those that have long passed for "objective truths." Or with Haraway's understanding of objectivity, which (she argues) is not about transcendence but about answerability:

> . . . not about dis-engagement, but about mutual *and* usually unequal structuring, about taking risks in a world where "we" are permanently mortal, that is, not in "final" control. . . .[41]

Accountability. The theology of the cross was and is profoundly relational. For Luther the relationship of God and humankind was, as I contended in Chapter 2, the framework of meaning, not only for theological discourse but also for humans' ultimate destiny and every dimension of their daily living, as individuals and in company with one another. We are always living "before" or "in the presence of" God (*coram Deo*). Simultaneously, we also live "before" or "in the presence of" the world of nature and other humans (*coram mundo*), a state of things made possible by and encompassed within our relationship with God. This notion is one of several signaling Luther's insight that our living is never solely a private matter—that whatever else may be said about it, it always also entails responding.

Accountability within an epistemology of the cross emerges from this background. This brief section is concerned with describing the several roles it plays.

(1) "A human being who is content with the world," Juan Luis Segundo claims, "will not have the least interest in unmasking the mechanisms that conceal the authentic reality."[42] An epistemology may be one way to maintain, if not create, contentment with the world, insofar as it functions as one of the mechanisms that conceal realities of exclusion and injustice. The critique an epistemology of the cross directs at epistemologies of glory expresses the insistence that account-

ability entails taking steps to become aware of such realities. In this sense, it is itself a demand for accountability.[43]

Among the most important dimensions of this critique is its insistence that knower and "knowee" are, in relation to one another and before God, *both* subjects and objects. To envision the knowing relationship as a nonreciprocal, "subject over against object" one is not only scientifically faulty but morally irresponsible.[44] An epistemology of the cross exercises a critique that is in the first instance a call for this sort of accountability.

(2) By the same token, this critique announces that an epistemology of the cross also requires accountability of itself. This is understood as acknowledgment of implication in and co-responsibility for the reality that privilege-based epistemologies, by design or not, conspire to conceal. Repeatedly, feminist epistemologies (particularly Haraway's work) remind us, almost in the same breath, that accountability is the epistemological value we must most passionately uphold—and that neither we as knowers, nor descriptions (as knowledge), nor the "practices" of knowledge-producing or -acquiring, are "innocent."

To acknowledge our individual and collective, and collaborative, lack of "innocence" (here in quotations to emphasize its many, sometimes paradoxical facets) means to confess: at the very least, that we *have* seen/that we *do* know; at the very most, that we have *done* something. Of course the object—*what* we have seen/*what* we do know/*what* we have done—makes an enormous difference, ethically; among other things, it may matter in terms of what we or others judge we must then do. But at the core of the matter is the plain fact that to name and recognize our lack of innocence is to describe ourselves as accountable for who we are and for what we know. An epistemology of the cross shares with feminist epistemologies a deep conviction that we are accountable "non-innocents."

123

(3) " . . . [T]he liberating function of theological understanding," Jon Sobrino observes,

> does not consist in explaining or giving meaning
> to an existing reality or to the faith as threatened
> by a particular situation, but in transforming a
> reality so that it may take on meaning and the lost
> or threatened meaning of the faith may thereby
> also be recovered. . . . [45]

Theology, in other words, cannot be separated from the
ethical and the practical—not only in its implications but
also in its sources and resources. If Sobrino is right (as he
alludes to Marx's criticism of Feuerbach), then those who
do theology are accountable: not to justify or bless what he
calls "the wretched state of the real world,"[46] but to change
it.[47]

An epistemology of the cross plays a key role in facili-
tating this transformational accountability: not only theologians' but also that of others committed to human dignity.
Feminist epistemologists began their critical work in response to insults and injustices generated—to paraphrase
Sobrino—by scientific and philosophical understandings that
"explained" and "gave meaning to existing realities" of exclusion. The tasks of "contestation" to and "deconstruction"
of these understandings continue; but they have been aug-
mented by "passionate construction, webbed connections,
and hope for transformation of systems of knowledge and
ways of seeing."[48] Accountability involves both critical *and*
creative, transformational work. If critical accountability's
project is the unmasking, then creative accountability's project
is proposing visions and gathering the handiworkers to
discuss, revise, and attempt to realize them.

An epistemology of the cross owes its view of the created
world to faith's conviction of the transformative solidarity of

God with the world. In enabling a clearer view of reality, in helping us recognize our implication in that reality, and in equipping us to participate, within and through God's transformative solidarity, to affirm human dignity within that reality, an epistemology of the cross both expresses and sustains its essential accountability.

How an Epistemology of the Cross Works

[handwritten margin note: heuristic - Eureka to find - metaphor.]

No epistemology, not even this one, can *make* knowing happen. An epistemology of the cross is a heuristic device, *[handwritten: Def.]* a conceptual tool, aimed to help describe one way of understanding the relationship between experience and knowledge. *[handwritten: of]* *[handwritten: "compelling"]* If it is intelligible, this proposal may help describe how it is that our lived experience may and sometimes does issue in "compelling knowledge," that is, knowledge that compels us to live accountably.

This process involves three parts: ① seeing or coming to know what is going on (or *that* something is going on); ② recognizing and comprehending one's own relation to or involvement in what is going on; and ③ doing something about what is going on. These three are not discrete or sequential events or stages. Instead they stand in dynamic relation to one another; they may even constitute one another.

We cannot recognize that we are involved, nor will we feel moved to act, if we do not see what is the case to begin with. Insofar as we do not believe ourselves implicated, we are unlikely to be moved to act. Having acted (when and if we do, and for whatever reasons) in a given situation, we *become* implicated, involved (even though we may move immediately to circumscribe or escape our involvement). The fact of our involvement may be just what is needed to draw our attention, sometimes for the first time, to what is really going on, who is really there, and even, if time and circumstances allow for it, to how it was that we never noticed any of this before.

In what follows, I will argue that an epistemology of the cross describes how it is that we may and sometimes do come to see what is the case; recognize our own implication in it; and feel compelled to act in a morally accountable way. The discussion will concentrate on the first two parts of this process, since they are more easily and perhaps more appropriately treated in epistemological terms.

If this proposal makes an effective, sensible argument, it will have practical, ethical implications: It will promote concern about, and alertness to, the elements that characterize the coming-to-know that compels a faithful response; it will also help knowers recognize what matters about it.

Dillusionment, or Coming to See What Is the Case

> Man hides his own things in order to deny them . . . .
>
> Martin Luther[49]

> . . . The most revolutionary act is and will always be, to say aloud what is.
>
> Rosa Luxemberg[50]

Beverly Harrison writes that the "the basic stance that precipitates [liberation] ethical reflection . . . [is] the power or capacity to be 'the subjects of our lives.'"[51] "Conscientization"—the awkward English version of the mellifluous Spanish *concientización*, or "coming to awareness"—is the "awakening" into that subject-hood, a process that begins but is never fully completed. An essential part of this awakening is a collective "naming" process.

Douglas John Hall's *Lighten Our Darkness*, published in 1976 and remarkably contemporary two decades later, begins with a thorough description and critique of a people who, caught up for generations in the ideologies of progress and the possibility of human mastery of nature and history, cannot now face the darkness of a contemporary reality in which these myths have fallen apart. These are people who seem always to have acted as if they were subjects of their lives; now, Hall argues, they do not have the eyes or the heart to manage the bitter discrepancy between the expectations the myth of unstoppable progress has fed and the experiences the twentieth century has served up. Privilege, not conscience, distinguishes these "subjects."

"We indulge our sense of expectancy," writes Hall,

> along lines so unqualifiedly positive that no negative, not death itself, can be seriously admitted at the conscious level. . . . [We seem to] have to look away from death in order to find the courage to live. . . . [52]

Many North American Christians are among these people who share the "problem of social myopia."[53] Instead of correcting the distortion, Christianity for its part has "function[ed] primarily as insulation. . . . "[54] The *conscientización*—an awakening to "critical consciousness"—needed by those unwilling or unable to face the experience of limits and its consequences for themselves and for others, is no less urgent than that needed by those who have been forced to the margins.

Individuals and societies deny, repress, paper over, and rewrite unbearable realities. The Holocaust has occasioned some of the most grievous attempts to bury atrocity.[55] Trauma in the form of domestic and sexual violence, combat in wartime, and political terror becomes unspeakable.[56] Death is denied, not only by the family that "loses" a loved one unexpectedly in a drive-by shooting, but also by a multi-million-dollar medical industry determined to discover what technology can do to thwart the weariness of a diseased heart or a comatose brain.[57] The connections between the price of a cup of coffee in New York City and the tenuousness of life for the children who pick the coffee beans four months a year in El Salvador or Brazil go unremarked millions of times each day.[58] Eager for relief from the daily irritations of the headlines' carefully interpreted "bad news," we wonder why the papers can't cover the *good* news more often.

Our inability, or refusal, to see what is the case is problematic for those individuals whose lives might be dignified or liberated—or at least, lived in less turmoil—if we could or would acknowledge the reality of their suffering. But it also has major implications for our lives together as a society—a society in which long-term denial of this sort leads to moral blindness, and blindness, to ethical incompetence and injustice. Those who suffer in such a society, and those to whose suffering such a society contributes at a distance, fade or are banished from sight, from consciousness, and therefore, from conscience. All are *not* here, not accounted for. With them, their suffering, its causes, and our shared implication in it, disappear as well. Under such circumstances, Rosa Luxemburg may have a point. But under the circumstances, who would want to commit "the most revolutionary act"? Who would want to say "what *is*"?

Planted in the midst of this picture, feminist critiques of traditional epistemologies begin to hum. Feminists' repeated warnings that no epistemological position, no knower, no framework, can claim "innocence" are bracing here; have we too often disguised our habitual ignorance of suffering reality as just such a childish claim: "We didn't know"? Does the existence of "one true story" in science or religion (and the public-address-system power to project it longer and louder than any other story) obviate the need—or even subvert the value—of searching out less attractive stories told by less booming voices? "The questions we choose to ask," writes Jantzen,

... do not occur to us out of the blue; they are
related to that which we consider it important or
interesting to know, and this is in turn to a very
great extent a function of our individual and corporate history. . . . [59]

The reality of a "dominant meaning system" that ignores the
experiences of certain groups—in particular the experiences
of suffering that are more often and more egregiously the
lot of marginalized groups than of privileged ones—has a
pervasive effect on the sensibilities and possibilities of even
the most conscientious individuals living within that system's
ambit. It is tough to avoid the impact; as Harding points
out, "The same kinds of social forces that shape the rest of
the world shape [us]." [60]

"The dominant tradition," Hall writes,

looks at the cross from the standpoint of its overcoming. It exists as a symbol of that which stood
in the way of human expectations, and which has
been set aside . . . . [61]

Whatever the cross once meant, how ever scandalous it once
may have been, this illusory "American-way-of-life" kind of
Christianity now lives uneasily with the assurance that all *that*
is long past, that "death has been swallowed up in victory"—
a disposition Hall identifies with what he calls "kerygmatic
triumphalism." The problem with this disposition is, he says,
that it makes it virtually impossible to take evil, the suffering
associated with it, and those who suffer, seriously:

If real evil has already been overcome, then the
evil that manifests itself in our actual existence
can only be regarded as unreal . . . Human responsibility . . . is virtually set aside. Reality becomes . . .

identified with the proclaimed triumph, and faith
is defined as the will to believe this triumph in
the face of all obstacles. . . . [62]

It may be that an epistemology of the cross describes
what happens when the "will to believe this triumph" fails,
and whatever "faith" was thought to be, it becomes un-
coupled from the bullet train to better days. A death not
anticipated, fought against; an encounter with traumatic
violence; a last, lost job; a prayer for another's deliverance,
not answered; a human face—perhaps a friend's—unexpectedly attached to the "threat" of AIDS; a sojourn to a
place or among a people where neither heart nor mind can
make sense of the suffering one sees: Any of these can be
the occasion on which the lights fail, and—for the longest
moment—neither success nor denial can restore them. Not
all but many of these occasions of personal suffering are
intimately woven into the dynamics of the larger society,
which allows or foments occasions of local and distant
suffering that are neither random nor unavoidable. Face to
face with these cross-shaped occasions, is it any wonder
that individuals and whole societies seek escape through
denial or blindness? That "faith" is redefined to refer to
something manageable, something that at least resembles
what we know we can count on?
An epistemology of the cross may attend to what Elizabeth A. Johnson calls that "fruitful experience" that occurs

when persons bump up against the stubborn resistance of historical reality to what they sense to
be true, good, and beautiful. When reality is thus
"dis-illusioning," the contrast challenges people to
a decision: either close their minds and deny what
they have experienced, or use it as a springboard
to address and struggle with the causes of the
suffering.[63]

An epistemology of the cross may attend to that moment when the illusions fall apart: not because we are clever or insightful enough to know an illusion when we see it, but because it will no longer hold, despite our best efforts. An epistemology of the cross may make note of our "dis-illusionment." There is little enjoyment or satisfaction in this coming-to-know; it seems rather to be an experience of almost painful clearness of sight. It is only part of the process of "call[ing] the thing what it actually is."[64]

Epistemological Conversion, or Recognizing One's Implication

> *Adam, [my father] would say, What is the fundamental question one must ask of the world? I would think of and posit many things, but the answer was always the same:* Why is the child crying? . . .
>
> Alice Walker[65]

" . . . Everyone is innocent until they arrive in El Salvador. . . . "[66]

You cannot *be* there until you *get* there. And you are not there until you arrive. And you have not really arrived until you begin to ask, "Why is the child crying?" And if you can wait to listen to the answer, or to the silence of no answer, you *are* there.

It is often difficult to say when the line is crossed between seeing what is going on and acknowledging rela-tionship, involvement, even implication in it. The more attentive one becomes to what is going on, the more one feels oneself "drawn in"—as one can be drawn, say, even into a painting at a museum or a poem read aloud.

We have already seen that feminist epistemologies reject the notion that the knower/subject is on a different (under-stood to be higher, advantageous) causal plane than the

131

knowee/object. One does not act on the other without reciprocity. The fact that subject and object inhabit the same causal plane—and that this is so often ignored—is one of the terms of reference that invests research design and outcomes with moral as well as scientific significance. To say the two parties involved occupy the same causal plane is to say that they affect one another; it also means that each has value.

The struggle to reconceptualize objectivity, as feminists have been at great pains to clarify, is necessary not only because there is moral virtue in reversing epistemological practices that contribute to injustice but also because there is scientific virtue in gathering more, and richer, evidence about how it is with the world, ourselves included. Feminist epistemological discussions of objectivity place great value on factors such as participatory values (Harding) and answerability (Haraway) that express wholehearted mutual involvement rather than the impassive, cool "over-against-ness" characteristic of traditional scientific notions of objectivity. Knowers work in groups; knowledge-making is a collective and collaborative activity. The story of the lone knower is an individualist fable, feminists argue, for even those who discover "alone" have relied on the work, good and bad, done before they knew what a slide rule or a computer was.

The more serious the conversation becomes about what is really going on (a rough-and-ready definition of objectivity, perhaps), the clearer it becomes that we are implicated with one another in our knowing. Among the modalities in which this mutual epistemological implication expresses itself are the ways in which we collaborate in and benefit from marginalizing one another. Even—perhaps especially—here, we are much more "in relation with" than "over against," as Harding illustrates:

> [S]houldn't one speak of majority "overadvantage"
> as the logical companion to minority "under-

advantage" or "disadvantage"? . . . [S]ome people probably get "too much justice"—that is, are unfairly favored by social institutions. It must be just as unjust for some to be the over-beneficiaries as it is for others to be the under-beneficiaries. . . . [67]

This is not to say that "justice" is a zero-sum game, but rather that we stand—in matters of social justice, as with the epistemological questions (like who qualifies as a knower) that play into our practices of justice—"in relation to" one another. We cannot avoid involvement.

What we do seem able to avoid is acceptance of our involvement.

Rooted in the faith-based conviction of God's solidary involvement with humankind as expressed in the incarnation, an epistemology of the cross helps us to recognize and accept our involvement. The cross, as Sobrino observes, is not the result of an ahistorical decision on God's part, but is rather "the outcome of the basic option for incarnation in a given situation[,] . . . the outcome of Jesus' historical path."[68] God's decision to participate in the broken world—a world we recognize as ours, too—comes to a kind of physical and historical breaking point on the cross. It is there we glimpse the stuff God is made of. God does not overpower the negative from the outside, Sobrino points out; "rather, on the cross we see God submerged *within* the negative," and it is there that the "possibility of overcoming the negative is realized."[69] In the first instance, though, it is the "being there" with the losers that, as we see it, scandalizes us and makes us wonder whether we have been running with the right God.

When we come face to face with similar scenarios patched together out of the lives of those among whom we live, we may respond as Welch did when as a member of a solidarity group she saw a film about the war in El Salvador. Until that point, her participation had been "fairly straightforward" and unproblematic; but

watching pictures of the police and the military
drag people into the streets[,] . . . hearing descriptions of tortured and mutilated bodies, feeling a
fraction of the horror of that situation, shattered
all my worlds of meaning.[70]

What happens when the "worlds of meaning" are shattered,
when the categories no longer work to make sense of what
one sees because one has decided to stand in a different
place? "One cannot relocate in any possible vantage point,"
Haraway writes, "without being accountable for that movement. Vision is *always* a question of the power to see . . . . With
whose blood were my eyes crafted?"[71] There is no way to
move without running into someone.

An epistemology of the cross is an attempt to describe,
not explain, how God's solidarity with the world underwrites our own solidarity with those on the margins. It
describes a shift in consciousness, and conscience,[72] from
the recognition that "everyone must be somewhere" (social
location) to the question, "Where must *I* be?" (moral accountability for social location); from the observation that
there is no neutral space to the conviction that I need to be
accountable for which space I am occupying. The homeless
panhandler and the soup-kitchen regular, the crack-addicted
and those who are dying of AIDS, the battered woman and
the chronically mentally ill,

[m]erely by being there, . . . call into question those
who approach, challenging their "being human";
and this radical questioning of what it means to be
a human being serves as the historical mediation of
our questioning of what "being God" means.[73]

Based on his own experience, Luther was sure that
people have a hard time letting God be God. Most of us are
busy, in one way or another, either making up the god we

134

want or need or (and often simultaneously) acting as our own god, in relation to ourselves and in relation to others. Luther also argued that the issues of "being human" and "being God" are wedded in the human consciousness. Face to face with another person with whom I do not particularly want to be associated or identified, let alone in solidarity with, I must find the question of what it means to be human difficult indeed. Have I here met my match, or my limit? The fact that I cannot disguise our "family resemblance"—how much this "outsider" and I resemble each other!—leads me to believe that I have met the limit of my well-polished definition of "being human," or of "human being," and it is too small and too mean. Even if I never get to the question of what "being God" means, the ongoing struggle to sort out this matter of being human—a struggle I share with those who "confront [me] with the God of the cross"[74]—may begin the work of an "epistemological conversion" in me. Yes, it matters whether I can or am willing to see what is going on. But I am still a spectator until I am enabled and willing to acknowledge my implication in what is going on.

Responsive Accountability, or
Knowing Oneself Compelled to Act

> Solidarity *is* accountability, and accountability means being vulnerable, capable of being changed by the oppressed, welcoming their capacity to critique and alter our reality.[75]

Harrison's definition of solidarity/accountability is not exhaustive, but it draws attention precisely to the state of readiness to which an epistemology of the cross draws us. It is a disconcerting state of readiness: vulnerable, mutable, disposed to hear criticism willingly, even to anticipate changes in "our way of life." On the whole, the characterization sounds like a invitation to passivity, not to action; it sounds like a prescription for weakness, not strength. Commended to the privileged, however, this definition of solidarity with the oppressed is a challenge that requires more work than most of us are willing to do, more strength than most of us have. It requires accountability that responds.

It requires, for example, that the critique that both feminists and an epistemology of the cross direct at power and power-epistemologies become in addition an exercise in *self*-criticism. For us as knowers, this is not an occasion for self-abnegation[76] (much less, for self-absorption) but for honesty—first with ourselves in our places of relative privilege, and then, too, with others: both the well-connected and the set-adrift. "Honest compassion is possible," writes Carter Heyward, "only where reality is actually named and dealt with."[77] It is a priority of any self-respecting liberatory epistemology that it "actually name and deal with" reality.

That this is a complicated and ongoing process, no one should doubt. Within and between our multiply identified, socially constructed selves, as we have seen, there are "parts" that are stigmatized, parts that are privileged; it is difficult to gain the clarity one might want, especially in trying to determine who is "right" and who is just talking louder than the rest. It is not an exact science, this sorting out. At the same time, in trying to determine what is more, and what is less, false—or even more right—the eye should be "on the sparrow": this is what Harrison's injunction calls for, and it is also what an epistemology of the cross suggests.

That active solidarity should in the first instance be a place of responsiveness, which may even include silence, is not strange—just surprising, perhaps. Dietrich Bonhoeffer, writing from his imprisonment by the Nazis, judged Christians (himself among them) unable to find "new and revolutionary" sense in the "traditional words and acts" borne in their religious heritage. "Our church," he wrote, " . . . has been fighting in these years only for its self-preservation."[78] Disqualified from speaking because of the incredibility of their previous speech, Bonhoeffer believes, Christian people must enter a period in which "being Christians . . . will be limited to two things: prayer and righteous action among men." Until renewal comes, "the Christian cause will be a silent and hidden affair. . . . "[79] Bonhoeffer's reflections underscore the need for *metanoia* that responds accountably.

Liberation theologians lift up the profound value of silence as part of the process of theologizing.[80] The silence of not speaking is also part of learning how to accompany those who suffer. Far from acquiescing in the causes or injustice of suffering, it is an undergirding, a sign of fellowship that may also be the first sign of solidarity in protest. It is not unrelated to the silence Bonhoeffer's observations commend.

A responsive but not passive state of readiness also entails that one should expect to live with ambiguity and instability: not only in the face of how things are, but also in anticipation of how things may be, as either our reality or our framework for interpreting reality changes. Harding observes that "[f]eminist analytical categories *should* be unstable—consistent and coherent theories in an unstable and incoherent world are obstacles to both our understanding and our social practices."[81] An epistemology of the cross resonates with this assessment.

We must also take uncertainty and doubt into account; at least intermittently, each of us must deal with them. For Welch, for example, there is a correlation between liberation faith, with its deepening "conversion to the other," and doubt as to the possibility of reconciliation. For her, faith may be at least in part "the courage to act and to think within an uncertain framework . . . , an acceptance of risk and openness"[82] like the one responsive accountability calls for.

Responsive accountability grows out of disillusionment and epistemological conversion; it also contributes to their ongoing accomplishment. Each part of the process that connects lived experience with accountable, faithful action depends on the rest. Finally, an epistemology of the cross, like its theological foundation, directs us to its hope in God's transformative solidarity with the world in its brokenness, and to the possibility that it may serve to guide our knowing and our doing so that "[our] love may overflow more and more with knowledge and full insight to help [us] determine what is best. . . ."[83]

One Last Word

I have used the word "affinities" to describe the concerns I have elaborated in Luther's theology of the cross and in feminist epistemologies. It is a term with considerably more magnetic energy than "coincidences," but less such energy than, say, "compelling (concerns)" would have. It seems to me that "affinities" is a fair and perhaps even an exciting descriptor—especially in light of the conversational possibilities I hope I have illuminated.

Luther's clarity about the proper subject and the limits of theology grants a great deal of freedom to explore some of the epistemological implications that can be drawn from the theology of the cross. It seems to me that Christian theologians and secular feminist philosophers might discover that they can talk with each other, after all, as the former make the attempt to de-mystify what can be de-mystified about knowing in Christian theology and faith, and the latter discover all is not shrouded in revelation.

The elements of an epistemology of the cross are as richly expressed in secular feminist philosophical terms as they are in terms "of the cross," but they are best expressed in the conversation between the two "interlocutors," even where one cannot or would not concur fully with the other. In its principal function—to describe the movement from lived experience to compelling knowledge, a movement that involves seeing what is the case; comprehending one's implication in it; and coming to accept accountability to act on what is known—such an epistemology facilitates a project as dependent on our collective sense of urgency as it is on our commitment and our willingness to hope.

In the Preface of this book, I posed a series of discomfiting questions, among them these: What have we not known, or not been willing to know? What have we refused to be accountable for? Who are those whose suffering we refuse to see, because we cannot live with our complicity in it? What can enable us to ask and answer these questions honestly? I hope that we have made some progress toward responding to these questions. But before congratulations are in order, a few more questions need to be raised. They take the form of formidable possible objections to an epistemology of the cross.

4

Objections

Assuming the proposal for an epistemology of the cross made in the previous chapter is reasonably sturdy in terms of argument and evidence, it may be that such a proposal is both possible and useful. However, there may be objections that, if they are weighty enough and well founded, may sink it anyway. At the very least, raising possible objections will have the salutary effect of provoking closer scrutiny of the proposal and greater circumspection in its use. To raise them here, before the discussion within these covers ends, is to exercise accountability, which has figured centrally in my treatment of both feminist epistemologies and an epistemology of the cross.

The two main objections to be explored have to do with privilege and with suffering. The first is articulated in the form of the following question: *Can a privileged church claim an epistemology of the cross?* This objection concerns itself with the extent to which a church that exercises privilege in local or global society has either the capacity or a moral right also to exercise a claim to an epistemology of the cross.[1] The second objection takes this form: *Does an epistemology of the cross glorify suffering?* This question deals with the capacity an epistemology of the cross has to promote or justify suffering for the sake of "compelling knowledge," and the probability that it will do so. Both objections are essentially moral; depending on how fundamental they turn out to be vis-à-vis the content of an epistemology of the cross, however, they may also raise questions about whether such an epistemology makes any sense. I would also reiterate here a point made at the beginning of the book, namely, that while both objections (but principally the first) focus on the misappropriation of the cross by a privileged church, an epistemology of the cross can be understood to have broad implications for individuals, groups, and societies in positions that allow them to abuse power.

These two particular, powerful objections to an epistemology of the cross are traceable directly to its reliance, even dependence, on the theology of the cross. It seems only fair that such an epistemology, insofar as it takes credit for the strengths of its chief resource, also be held to account for the liabilities that resource may bring with it. A historical review of theologies of the cross that includes Luther's may be said to begin with Paul's epistles and the gospel writers' accounts of the passion story, and to encompass as well a great variety of theories about atonement shaped "in the language and thought that people of a particular time understood and in which they were grounded."[2] Such an historical review can instruct us—though it is unlikely to bring in a final determination—on where Christian talk about and use of the cross have gone wrong and are likely to go wrong, and what happens when they do.

Much of contemporary debate about the theology of the cross and atonement theories responds to what Elisabeth Schüssler Fiorenza terms the "preconstructed 'common-sense' meanings" of "doctrinal discourses of redemption and salvation . . . deeply ingrained in Christian consciousness."[3] To the extent this is true, it is debate as to whether we have misinterpreted the truth as Paul or Anselm or Luther, or any other theologian writing about the cross of Christ, may have seen it. Is the cross really about atonement, or about at-one-ment? Is it about God's divine plan to send the Son as a ransom? Is it about the Father-God's [sic] intentional, bloody sacrifice of his [sic] only son so that we humans might live forever in heaven? Is it an "insult to God" that is then (in the resurrection) redeemed by the One who gives life? Is it the inevitable outcome of incarnation and/or a life of ministry with and among the outcast? Proof of divine solidarity with human suffering?

The arguments made to object to an epistemology of the cross will probably look and sound somewhat like those made to object to the theology of the cross. "The cross," not "epistemology," is more likely to generate whatever reservations appear. Elements of the contemporary debate about the meaning and importance of the cross in Christian doctrine are bound to enter into discussions of the two objections I have suggested to an epistemology of the cross; however, in-depth coverage of that debate is far beyond the scope of this chapter and this book. In my replies, I will rely here, as I did in drafting the proposal for an epistemology of the cross itself, on the interpretation of Luther's theology of the cross as laid out in the second chapter.

The two objections I have raised are intimately related to one another. "Privilege" usually implies power; a good deal of the time, as Fiddes observes, " . . . this world . . . understands power to be the ability to inflict suffering, or at least to escape from it."[4] Historically, the political and economic privilege/power of Christendom, or of the church itself, has been the vehicle as well as the justification for inflicting suffering, whether or not the church has acknowledged it as such. Historically, the privileged have always been in favored positions to name and define the aims and the consequences of their projects.

The privileged church has rarely defined the aims of projects like "evangelization," "mission," and "good order" in terms of suffering; when suffering has resulted, however, this church has had a virtually chronic penchant for blessing or justifying it, or for ignoring or renaming it, for the sake of a church-defined "greater good." The objection that an epistemology of the cross may glorify suffering arises at this point. It is raised by or in the midst of those who suffer, and takes their lived experience of suffering as morally and epistemologically authoritative. It neither tolerates blaming the victims of inflicted suffering nor assumes that suffering is an ethically indifferent matter.

The question of whether a privileged church has the right to lay claim to an epistemology of the cross usually arises out of moral indignation at the discrepancy between what the church says it believes and what it evidently practices; the serious theological question of what the church actually *is* complicates matters. The distance—if and when it is noticed—between what the church says it is and/or aspires to, and what the church actually does, has often been rationalized by recourse to theological reflections about original sin and the congenital human propensity to fall short of the glory of God.

When this occurs, daily tragedies of human sufferers are "swallowed up": not in the victory of resurrection, but in a triumphalistic and privileged church's self-justifying talk about resurrection. Theology then thinly veils ideology, enabling such reflections to cover and excuse a multitude of sins and obviating the value and significance of repentance, forgiveness, and faithful constructive or reparative action. In these cases it may be that the tradition itself not very subtly undermines the cogency of an epistemology of the cross.

Either of these intertwined objections would itself be worth a book. Existing resources on each draw together an enormous relevant body of literature that is by no means exclusively theological. In what follows I will attempt modestly but sharply to spell out and respond to each in the awareness and with the hope that what begins here will lead to more extensive conversation.

Can a Privileged Church Claim an
Epistemology of the Cross?

... [T]he theology of the cross ... could be either
a blessing or a curse. It all depends on who is
talking about the theology of the cross, to whom
it is addressed, and whose interests it intends
serving.[5]

To ask whether a privileged church can claim an epistemology of the cross clearly implies some doubt about the
matter. That it implies this but does not entirely rule out a
claim reflects the problematic character of the issue at the
heart of the question.

As we have seen, Luther's theology of the cross, which
provides the rootage for an epistemology of the cross, was
in the first instance a scathing critique of what he called the
"theology of glory," produced by a privileged, powerful,
and self-justifying church. Luther seemed to say that it is all
but in the nature of such a church to generate such a
theology; the institution reflects both humans' compulsion
to create God in their own image, and their utter incapacity
to see themselves as creatures made in God's image—an
image, Luther argued, that humans can see only in God's
self-revelation in Jesus on the cross.

Von Loewenich has written that " ... the Lutheran
church ... surrendered Luther's theology of the cross far too
quickly," that "[t]he theology of glory that Luther opposed ...
made a triumphal entry also into his church."[6] I have
relied on Luther's theology of the cross to inform an
epistemology that, as it lights the way toward morally
responsible knowing, refuses self-consciously to be taken
in by the blandishments of power and privilege; opts for
the relative authoritativeness of the perspective of the
marginalized; and expects and lives with limits, ambiguities, and doubts.

Does it make any sense to set these two sentences next to one another? The first acknowledges the rapid and ongoing betrayal of this theology's most acute insights by a part of the "universal" church that shares with, and may therefore stand in for, many others in positions of relative social, economic, and political privilege. The second asserts, from a position within that privileged church, that this theology may still empower those who seek to "disillusion" the privileged and call them/us to responsive account. These are, respectively, the "indictment" and "response" in terms of which I will treat the first objection.

Indictment

African theologian Jean-Marc Éla writes that " . . . Martin Luther seems to have locked up the theology of the cross in the temples." He continues:

> In opposing the scandal of the cross to justifica-
> tion through the works of the law . . . [his theol-
> ogy becomes] [a]bsorbed . . . by the problem of
> individual salvation [and] . . . proves incapable
> of bringing out the critical and liberating power of
> the cross.[7]

We cannot say how Luther would have responded to the late-twentieth-century attack on a "passion without redemption" that fuels Éla's critique. Nearly five hundred years ago, however, Luther seems not to have drawn any sympathetic implications from his exposition of a theology of the cross in Heidelberg for the struggle of peasants, crushed by their rulers with Luther's enthusiastic support seven years there-after.[8] During these same years, half a planet away, the Spaniard Fray Bartolomé de las Casas (1484–1566) experienced what modern liberation theologians would call a "conversion to the poor" and took the battle to both Church and Crown to defend the "Indians" his countrymen were subjugating, sword in hand and cross in tow.[9]

A privileged church is in a position to turn historical crosses (sometimes of its own imposing) into occasions for those being crucified—the poor, the marginalized, women, children, and men—to "share in the suffering of Christ." When a privileged church interprets others' suffering in this way, the cross becomes for those who suffer less "a symbol of suffering [than] of the church's pride and arrogance."[10] Its act of interpretation is a theological exercise in the power of naming, which is secured by its starker political and economic forms. The cross becomes what Asian theologian C. S. Song calls "a theological construct unrelated to the realities of life and history."[11] If the cross can become a theological construct, then a theology of the cross can become (principally) "a way of making a distinction"—between one understanding of (the theological construct of) justification and another.[12] To sever the cross of Jesus Christ from history is to drain it of its reality for those, then and now, with whom history is occupied—those with whom the life and death of Jesus had and has to do. The theology of the cross (which indeed is and was, among other things, a theological construct) was Luther's attempt to describe something that went far beyond a mere construct: namely, his/a believer's lived experience of what we might now call existential negation and divine graciousness.

The power of privilege (and the privilege of power) can often be measured by how deftly and thoroughly those who exercise it transcribe reality, wittingly or unwittingly, into terms that suit them. Hall describes some of the consequences of such transcriptions in North American churches:

> . . . [B]usiness and professional people, whose whole life centers around the ideas of work, effort, and mastery, singing hymns about the total dependence of man and the futility of his work!

> Persons [with] office, wealth, and power in their
> communities, listening to such readings as I Cor.,
> chs. 1 and 2: "Not many of you were wise accord-
> ing to worldly standards . . . but God chose what
> is foolish in the world to shame the wise. . . ." The
> irony is . . . these scenes . . . are not . . . experienced
> as . . . ironic.[13]

Such "ludicrous scenes," as Hall calls them, are precise
counterparts to solemn churchly exhortations to battered
women, or to people of color in racist societies, to "carry
their cross of suffering with dignity and without complaint
as Jesus Christ carried his."[14] The problem is not only theological; it is epistemological, and brings with it the ethical
freight knowing/not knowing always does: an unwillingness—and (perhaps) an intrinsic human incapacity—to see
what is the case, especially when seeing what is the case
may cook one's own plump goose.

In the hands of the relatively privileged, the unbrutalized,
how can a symbol of brutal execution, and the theology
that reflects on its meaning in the contemporary context,
escape reduction to an abstraction, a "theological idea"?
Only with great difficulty, if at all. Éla indicts theologies
elaborated by Europeans and North Americans; as the church
grows in numbers and in theological voice throughout the
world, he argues, such theologies, unrelated to the real,
lived scandal of the cross, are less and less assured of
remaining "the official theology of the entire church." For
Éla, as for many of his liberation-theological colleagues in
Africa, Asia, Latin America, and North America, the irony is
that those who have promulgated the theology (of the cross)
have also collaborated in recreating the scandal it (the cross)
refers to—and seem unable to see that they have done so.

> A sort of specific suffering [accompanies] . . .
> Western expansion beyond its frontiers. Depriva-

tion of one's own self, massacres, annihilation of indigenous cultures, systems of exclusion or destruction . . . belong to [the] . . . savagery that the West carries along with itself from a "culture of intolerance and violence" that belongs intrinsically to it.[15]

Certainly the sorts of suffering Éla lists also involve many *within* the West's own "culture of intolerance and violence," a culture so often smugly identified as "Christian." As North American feminists Joanne Carlson Brown and Rebecca Parker note, for example, "Christianity has been a primary—in many women's lives *the* primary—force in shaping our acceptance of abuse." They continue:

The central image of Christ on the cross as savior of the world communicates . . . that suffering is redemptive. If the best person who ever lived gave his life for others, then, to be of value we should likewise sacrifice ourselves. . . . Those . . . shaped by the Christian tradition feel that self-sacrifice and obedience are not only virtues but the definition of a faithful identity."[16]

Privilege permits the creation and reification of distortions that marginalization does not, though the marginalized who live within a system rationalized by these distortions may themselves also internalize them. Self-sacrifice, humility, obedience, and suffering—especially when they are required of those who are in positions to have things required of them, do not threaten privilege; idealizing these attributes (especially for women and others who "serve"), and associating them with Jesus, have never "cost" much. At all events, these are not and have never been qualities valued by captains of industry or political movers and shakers. No wonder the cross hovers comfortably as a "theological construct" in the air of abstraction. Perhaps an epistemology rooted in the theology of the cross is subject to the same manipulations as the *theologia crucis* itself.

Hall has suggested that "we" (North American, white, privileged Christians) have an almost incorrigible propensity "to regard the Christian gospel from a triumphalistic point of view .... There is something about the Christian message that seems to demand its being given the last word."[17] Here, it is difficult to separate two elements, both of which contribute to triumphalism: on the one hand, the effect of a perhaps understandable human desire to escape the scene of crucifixion—or a cruciform reality—for the sweet light of Easter; on the other, the impact of a comfortable, "our-way-of-life" kind of Christian-ism that has taught us, among other things, that there is no need to escape what we do not have to experience.

The triumphalism inspired by an individual's career ambitions realized and a nation's battles won becomes a too easy analogue for the triumph the gospel relates through life and death—and resurrection. The problem is, this sort of analogical thinking does not work—not when the world the gospel speaks to genuinely wonders what it is speaking about. For the privileged, on the other hand, there seems to be more "already" than "not yet," more resurrection than crucifixion: fertile ground for cultivating a theology of glory and its counterpart, an epistemology of glory.

Response

In a real sense, the question is not whether a privileged church *can* claim an epistemology of the cross. It *does* (at least, to the degree that it claims a theology of the cross). The question is, *how* can it?

"We need another kind of knowing," writes Fiddes, something that drives those of us who can afford an epistemology of glory beyond the "theological construct"—to the heart of what it means to know from the foot of the cross.[18] It may be that an epistemology of the cross is something only a privileged church *needs*; only a privileged church needs to come to terms with its illusions. It might begin, Hall observes, with its fantasy-images of the "pre-crucified Jesus of Hofmann's *Christ in Gethsemane* [or] . . . the post-crucified Christ-with-halo who stands at the door and knocks"; their iconography conveys a message with "all the depth of a singing commercial."[19] Until they are supplanted by clearer pictures, preached, painted, *known,* of a crucified Christ—"mutilated, sorrowful, forsaken"—

> there will be no facing up to the mutilation, sorrow, and forsakenness that this continent and its European satellites visit upon millions of the poor, including our own poor. Nor will there be any confrontation with the sickness within the soul of this society which causes it to seek the enemy outside its own soul.[20]

Those outside the North American context, whose voices figure so prominently and justifiably in the "indictment" above, offer counsel to those they accuse. The cross is imposed on—but it can also be *taken up by*—those who "challenge the . . . structures that abuse the people created in the image of God."[21] The cross is certainly an expression of inhumanity; it is also, however, an expression of the most profound humanity: "the end result of a . . . life that challenges the systems . . . of oppression . . . in solidarity with . . . those who live on the periphery."[22] That is to say, it is possible to be and to act in concert with those who suffer; it is possible to use one's privilege, or dispense with it, in solidarity with the outsider.

An epistemology of the cross can equip those who take it seriously to respond to "one of the main tasks of a Christian community in solidarity with the impoverished,"

namely, "to contribute to the rebirth of sensitivity to suffering, of hope in the midst of hopelessness, frustration, and
discouragement."[23] In this sense, such an epistemology may
function penitentially (as Altmann argues liberation theology
does), not only toward those who have been most evidently
sinned against, but also in its effect on those who have
sinned most egregiously. In the former case, a framework
of knowing informed by the cross will require and enable
reparation and restoration; in the latter, humility, modesty,
a sense of limits, which may also enable reparation and
restoration of what is fitting.

Will a privileged church be able to claim such an
epistemology? This politically and theologically complicated
question has no simple answer. Those of us who comprise
the "privileged church" in this society are not only white
and male, middle-strata and heterosexual, health-insured and
married: those overdetermined (but even so, not guaran-
teed) to be "privileged." "We" are a multiply-identified con-
gregation; many of us are the "outsiders-within" whom Patricia
Hill Collins and bell hooks describe. Even within our individual selves, "we" struggle to cope with and give expression to identities that are sometimes at odds with one another
and often unrecognized or unwanted by the society within
which we are. "We" war with and contribute to our church;
we rebel against the traditions of our faith, and yet are their
next steps. Even when we condemn and confess the sins of
racism, sexism, heterosexism, classism, imperialism, rapa-
cious capitalism, triumphalistic Christian-ism, and the like,
we remain oblivious to countless "small" sins all these ru-
brics encompass that we commit against one another each
day. God help us. No one is innocent.

But then, establishing innocence is not the theological
point—any more than being right is the epistemological one
(the two are sometimes confused with one another). Neither
a theology nor an epistemology of the cross aims to accom-
plish either goal. An epistemology of the cross seeks to

clarify and to convict, to valorize accountability and enable its realization. Those who want to appropriate a framework that helps do these things may have to suffer redrawing of the usual categories, recasting of the usual roles, and re-thinking of the usual truths. It is "another kind of knowing" (Fiddes) that a privileged church must prepare itself for.

Does an Epistemology of the Cross Glorify Suffering?

It has been said that the theology of the cross glorifies suffering. At the beginning of this chapter, I suggested that one of the marks of those who are privileged is that they are relatively well positioned to avoid suffering; another is a not altogether unrelated capacity they have to deny or ignore suffering. When forced to face the suffering of others, particularly those in whose suffering they may be complicit, the privileged may demonstrate a facility to interpret suffering in ways that exonerate themselves and/or make the sufferer, God, or human nature (their own possibly excepted) culpable. It is in interpreting suffering that the theology of the cross has served most commonly to "glorify" suffering; to champion the "value" of suffering (the concept) is to protect both God and those who cause, benefit from, and/or manage to escape suffering, one way or another. It also ignores the sufferer, from whose perspective and on whose behalf this objection arises.

The central symbol and theological focus in Christian theology and worship, the cross appears front and center in most Christian churches. "In the cross of Christ . . . ," we sing, ". . . I glory"; we often appear to worship the cross rather than the One whose life and ministry led to this brutal and humiliating destination. Those who have cared to do so have had few qualms about recruiting the theology of the cross to construe suffering to their taste: as acceptable, justifiable, to be borne without protest, blessed, deserved, inevitable. Suffering may be understood to be "acceptable" or "inevitable," the reasoning goes, because not much can be done, in any case, about suffering as a fact of human life; "justifiable," because humans as fallen creatures are getting their just desserts; "to be borne without protest," because that is how (we are told) the Divine Sufferer, Jesus, responded to his (undeserved) suffering[24]; "blessed," because suffering presumably provides the sufferer a chance to gain points with God by emulating Jesus; "deserved," because a particular person, or class of people, has provoked or brings suffering on themselves. If one of these characterizations springs a leak, another can and usually does bail it out. The net of such interpretations catches virtually all the fish it is meant to catch.

Luther's understanding of suffering occurs in light of the theology of the cross; it is woven into Luther's lived experience at every turn.[25] For Luther, according to von Loewenich,

> [t]he meaning of the cross does not disclose itself in contemplative thought but only in suffering experience . . . . Luther . . . practiced this theology in the face of death . . . . [E]very sentence is soaked with his heart's blood.[26]

It is terribly important to recognize here, as we have at several other points in discussing Luther's theology, that his emphasis on suffering as the form of true Christian discipleship is descriptive, *not* prescriptive, legalistic, or moralistic. It is also paradoxical, as is so much of his work; while gaining insights and articulating them in lecture, sermon, pamphlet, or conversation requires rigorous reasoning and clarity of thought, the truthfulness of what is articulated is revealed only to and in faith. These observations explain much of the susceptibility of Luther's insights to theological and psychological distortion. Although they certainly do not resolve the matter of whether Luther's perspective on suffering was right in his time or is right in ours, they do help to eliminate the basis for gross misuse of Luther's positions in contemporary arguments.

Luther had no use for self-chosen sufferings or suffering as good works; instead, he saw suffering in terms of "conformation" to Christ.[27] For Luther, von Loewenich writes, "[t]o be conformed to Christ means nothing else but experiencing the fact of the cross also in our lives," something God makes happen, and we apprehend in faith.[28] "The fact of the cross" may mean many things, but for Luther it surely included suffering, both in apprehending our own profound, existential "non-God-ness" and in experiencing the world's compulsive rejection of precisely what gives us life, namely, the gospel. Although we can have a rough idea what Luther, in his own time and place, may have pointed to as instances of these "inner" and "outer" sufferings,[29] they might very well take different forms in contemporary times and places.

"Every acceptance of suffering," writes Sölle, "is an acceptance of that which exists. The denial of every form of suffering can result in a flight from reality . . . ."[30] I believe that Luther's theological and existential concern with "the fact of the cross" in daily life was based in an "acceptance of that which exists," a constitutive part of the "right use of reality" Ebeling signals as the aim of (and the grounds for) Luther's theology of the cross. In this sense, Luther was no more interested in glorifying suffering than liberation theologians are in promoting grinding poverty when they insist that God is to be found particularly among the poor.

Much of what matters most in discussions of suffering—including the matter of whether or not it is being "glorified"—has to do with where and with whom one stands when one speaks. For those who are in a position to avoid suffering, it is infinitely easier to look *at* and talk *about* suffering than it is to enter *into* (or make oneself vulnerable to[31]) and speak out *from within* it. Those who prefer the panoramic view of suffering have been known to disparage the inside view as relativistic or subjective; it might make more sense to call it grounded, something all discussions of suffering have a moral obligation to be. The reality that what one sees (say, God's presence) has to do with where one stands (say, in suffering or in solidarity with those who suffer) tends to be the reality that observer-commentators do not want to see, the place they/we do not want to be, theologians of glory that they/we tend to be.

To spiritualize suffering or treat it as an abstraction is to deny its meaning and its weight. To learn to see it, and risk experiencing it, we must pay attention to the real world in which it occurs, to those who suffer, and to those, including ourselves, who are complicit. To sharpen this focus on suffering is not to glorify it, but rather to notice it and name it. Noticing and naming are essential parts of a larger and ongoing program: the determination to overcome suffering. For those who suffer, the first step, Sölle writes, "is . . . to find a language that . . . at least says what the situation is. . . ."[32] For those who begin truly to notice and name, to be *moved* by the suffering of others, ". . . the issue is not the truth or formal beauty" an theological or social scientific analysis of suffering might reflect; rather, as Sobrino observes, the issue is protest and "the elimination of the suffering."[33]

It is a terrible business, this coming to awareness of suffering. It is terrible existentially because coming to awareness of suffering brings suffering with it. It is terrible, too, because coming to awareness does mean full acceptance of its reality and, at the same time, full commitment to its elimination: and neither the acceptance nor the commitment can be relinquished, at least not this side of the eschaton. For people of privilege, reflections by Welch and Bonhoeffer may represent two moments within the heart that begins to be aware. Attending to the "voices of all who suffer and die without relief," Welch cautions that

[a]wareness of human suffering . . . carries with it
the danger of madness and the frightening con-
clusion that even if we win now, even if injustice
is eradicated, something irretrievable has been
lost.[34]

Her stark observation points out that what we say and do
often—perhaps usually—pales in the presence of actual
suffering. If we commit ourselves truly to correspond to
human suffering, we must take the risk to "be silenced or
at least chastised" in its presence.[35] Much if not most of the
time, it is simply not clear what suffering—our own or
others'—"means," or whether it means anything that we
hope, wish, or declare it to mean. We are hard-pressed to
answer the question, ". . . [H]ow can we give meaning to
suffering without sanctioning it?"[36] Always, we are better
advised to be silent on this score than to engage in facile
interpretation that may sanction suffering.

Shortly before his arrest by the Gestapo in 1943,
Bonhoeffer wrote these words:

We have to learn that personal suffering is a more
effective way, a more rewarding principle for
exploring the world in thought and action than
personal good fortune. . . .[37]

Bonhoeffer, traitor and patriot, felt anything but heroic. His
words were and are a sobering exhortation—even a self-
exhortation—drawn out of his own life's experience; they
are not a general letter of reference on behalf of suffering.
"Are we still of any use?" he wondered, without a trace of
cynicism.[38] Triumphalism, which includes the comfort of
belief in a God who guarantees meaning from the outset,
is set aside. Truly, "[s]uffering . . . ruptures our categories . . .
[and] demands a new paradigm for interpreting existence
and Christian witness."[39]

These last few pages argue implicitly that, as has been suggested earlier, Luther's theology of the cross has a profound epistemological dimension—here, vis-à-vis suffering. Siirala observes that "Luther speaks of the theology of the cross as a way of thinking which teaches one to [be] . . .

> open to things . . . contrary to [one's] own attitude. When a man barricades himself behind positions furnished by his own knowledge of good and evil, he selects as the content of his thought only those elements of reality that fit into the world created by his knowledge. . . . Only thinking which faces up to the cruciform nature of reality remains open to reality."[40]

An epistemology of the cross is inherently critical of the privilege and power that seem to allow the construction of barricaded positions from which some act in their own favor at others' expense and then rename others' suffering so that it disappears from view or ought to be welcomed by the sufferers.

An epistemology of the cross, moreover, authorizes lived experience: that of those who suffer, especially and in the first place; but also that of those relatively protected from suffering who begin to "face up to the cruciform nature of reality." Here we may recall the feminist epistemologies' commitments to the "standpoints of the subjugated" (Haraway) and the "perspective of the dominated" (Harding) on the dual grounds that these people, especially the women among them, have been unjustly excluded, to their great detriment, and that those at the margins have a better chance of giving a clearer account of how things really are than those in privileged positions have. Such commitments are intensified (again, even more so in the case of suffering) by the recognition that we are accountable—to others, and to one another—in and for what we know and what we do about what we know.

If there *is* "modest meaning in suffering" (Haraway), we may come to know what it is as part of the struggle of coming to see, to accept, and to overcome suffering. An epistemology of the cross, far from glorifying suffering, may prove to be a valuable conceptual tool in bringing into clearer focus a reality in which the privileged ignore or rename suffering too often, and bear with and protest it too seldom. ". . . [A]s long as Christ lives and is remembered, his friends will be with those who suffer," writes Sölle:

> Where no help is possible he appears not as a superior helper but only as the one who walks with those beyond help. That one bear the burden of the other is the simple and clear call that comes from all suffering.[41]

Conclusion

When the chips are down, the persuasiveness of an epistemology of the cross hinges not only on the aptness and "fit" of its principal resources; not only on the reasonableness and breadth of the framework, its elements and operation; not only on its capacity to respond satisfactorily to key objections.

In my judgment, an epistemology of the cross can claim to be a truly persuasive proposal only when it shows that it "works" when the rubber hits the road. The principal task of this book has been to lay the foundations and explicate the elements of this approach, not to demonstrate it in action. However, I would like briefly to show how elements of an epistemology of the cross might be used in real life, especially to suggest what sorts and sources of knowing are most crucial and what knowers' roles involve.

An Illustration

In her examination of suffering, Dorothee Sölle wonders, " . . . [W]here . . . is [it] that the crucifixion is happening to-day?"[1] There is no shortage of correct responses. One of them is psychological trauma—sexual and physical abuse, political terror and torture, wartime combat. I would argue that an epistemology of the cross as this book has proposed it could inform our understanding of and response to such trauma. For purposes of illustration, I rely on Judith Lewis Herman's description of trauma in *Trauma and Recovery* and her approach to studying and treating it.

People resist recognizing and speaking of atrocities. For individuals and whole societies, Herman contends, such "terrible events," even when they are allowed to enter consciousness, are often "unspeakable." The suffering psychological trauma causes is no less real, no less damaging to individuals as well as the relationships, groups, and communities they participate in, because of the illusion that such trauma does not occur, for example, in "our family" or among "our kind of people."

The destructive impact of psychological trauma, often accompanied by physical violence, has been called by other names, of which "hysteria" was probably the most common. In the late nineteenth century, Jean-Martin Charcot, his admirer Sigmund Freud, and a number of their contemporaries who treated female patients for grave psychological and (sometimes) somatic symptoms, listened over long periods of time to their recollections and then hypothesized that the childhood sexual and physical abuse they recalled had caused the symptoms from which these women now sought relief. Freud and others' initial commitments to call the thing by its right name suffocated in a political and social climate in which recognition of men's culpability for the "private" abuse of women and children threatened the patriarchal "good order" far more than did the effects of the abuse themselves.

Support for the victims of such trauma entails critique of privileged knowers, those who "know best" in the home and in society, and the sort of knowing they legitimate: for example, that men are entitled or at least "naturally" inclined to dominate "their" women. In historically, politically, and interpersonally supportive contexts, however, it becomes possible to call the damage psychological trauma does by its right name—Herman calls it "complex post-traumatic stress disorder"—or by any name at all. Naming is

> an essential step toward granting [survivors] . . . a measure of the recognition they deserve. It is an attempt to find a language that is at once faithful to the traditions of accurate psychological observation and to the moral demands of traumatized people. It is an attempt to learn from survivors, who understand, more profoundly than any investigator, the effects of captivity.[2]

All commitment to knowing is utterly entwined with being able and willing to see and to name.[3] It is also morally freighted. Commitment to knowing about and treating the effects of psychological trauma may require an approach that responds to and learns from those who have been hurt and have also been silenced—by perpetrators, but also by family members, friends, clergy, and others in a society that still would rather not know than share the suffering and the responsibility for knowing and transforming its causes.

An effective therapeutic process will depend, among other things, on the reconstruction of the story of what actually happened. But the therapist's role here is not that of an objective, scientific "fact-finder"; rather, she is to be an open-minded, compassionate witness whose principal concern and greatest personal challenge are to affirm "a position of moral solidarity with the survivor."[4] The integrity of the therapist is evidently crucial. Herman defines "integrity" eloquently—and aptly, in the context of this book—as

> the capacity to affirm the value of life in the face of death, to be reconciled with the finite limits of one's own life and the tragic limitations of the

human condition, and to accept these realities without despair.[5]

For the therapist, whose training and professional milieu grant scientific knowledge substantial value, "objectivity" cannot be value-neutral; instead, it involves finding the theoretical and therapeutic language that refuses to sacrifice ethical commitment. The search for that language, a project therapist and survivor plan and pursue jointly, requires the therapist to "bear witness" and, in doing so, to give up moral neutrality; "the bystander," Herman writes—in this case, the therapist—"is forced to take sides."[6]

In the ongoing encounter with the traumatized survivor, therapists "[must] . . . come to terms with their own capacity for evil . . . "[7] as well as the limits of their capacity to facilitate healing; these are dimensions to human being the therapist comes to realize she shares with others, especially in facing, with the survivor, her memories, suffering, and determination to come to terms with a bitter past. Finally,

> [t]he therapist . . . identifies with the patient through the experience of profound grief. The therapist may feel as though she herself is in mourning . . . . Unless [she] has adequate support to bear this grief, she will not be able to fulfill her promise to bear witness. . . .[8]

This account of psychological trauma and its terrible impact on the lives of children and adults explicates the extraordinary damage done when power-as-domination is abused. Self-knowledge, for example, is often constructed under conditions shaped by abusive power; sometimes it may also be *re*constructed, with great care and under conditions that protect, dignify, and empower.

Trauma and its treatment entail the centrality of embodied, lived experience in shaping our coming-to-know.

164

Again, both trauma and the treatment of it remind us repeatedly of our limits and vulnerability, and of the partial, ambiguous, and often problematic nature of our interpretations of our experience. Those who work with survivors, however, and survivors who engage in the struggle to recover their sense of wholeness, often discover through this regenerative process that what they come to know from the margins is knowledge of the most reliable and most valuable sort. "The fundamental premise of the psychotherapeutic work," Herman observes, "is a belief in the restorative power of truth-telling."[9] The process by which one comes to embrace this belief involves taking substantial risks in the face of great odds and with a profound sense of moral accountability, to oneself and to others.[10]

A Concluding Word

Knowing is an activity that requires participation and demands both commitment and judgment from the knower. Polanyi aptly characterizes the process of justifying beliefs—what makes it possible to claim that one knows something—as having a "fiduciary" character, even with respect to oneself as knower.[11] The process, he says, involves both recognition that knowing is always my (or another someone's) personal knowing, and trust that the basis I have for alleging knowledge is reasonable enough to authorize my claiming it.

But knowing also has a larger-than-personal context, which is significant not only epistemologically (in terms of justifying beliefs) but also ethically, as this book has argued throughout. An epistemology, understood as a framework or a lens, does not determine our individual or corporate ethical choices, but a particular epistemological framework (say, an epistemology of the cross) may narrow, broaden, enhance, deepen, or focus attention to and (therefore) knowledge of what is in such a way that we are enabled or even compelled to act responsively and in ways we believe we need to act to live faithfully.[12] Another epistemology would likely have other, perhaps quite different, implications for making both knowledge and ethical decisions based on it.

For the wider, interpersonal and societal context, the term "fiduciary" requires more plasticity and greater ethical substance; it surely characterizes the mode of knowing an epistemology of the cross authorizes, a mode J. Louis Martyn describes as *kata stauron*, or "according to the cross." This "new way of knowing," he writes,

> is not in some ethereal sense a spiritual way of knowing, . . . effected in a mystic trance . . . but rather right in the midst of rough-and-tumble life . . . . Seeing in a partial way has not yet been replaced by seeing face to face . . . [but rather] by faith.[13]

Faith underwrites an epistemology of the cross, makes it workable; it is the existential mode and medium this framework describes.

In this time in the United States, looking at the way the world is "known" is at the center of many political, economic, religious, and other systems and struggles. It is important to do this openly and to challenge the dominant distribution of power. In particular, the connection between social and theological epistemologies, and between any truly useful epistemology and its ethical freightedness, must be articulated as a challenge within institutions that prefer their own views of God and of power. To pose such a challenge explicitly has been part of the agenda of this book.

"What kinds of knowledge about the empirical world do we need," Harding asks, "in order to live at all, and to live more reasonably with one another on this planet from this moment on?"[14] Is it "facts" that are not known? Or is the problem that we do not know where to look, whom to listen to? What sort of knowing do we lack? From whom, and how, do we learn what we need to know? How do we face and let go of our resistance to the sort of knowing we must practice if we are to live faithful lives?

These are epistemological questions awakened, not by a concern about whether knowledge is possible, or whether it can be certain, but by a concern about the role knowing and knowers play in obstructing or fomenting liberating change. These are the kinds of questions to which an epistemology of the cross wants to respond.

Notes

Preface

1. "Compelling" as used here, as in the title, has a positive connotation, suggesting "irresistible" or "persuasive." It is not meant to have the negative connotations associated with "compulsive" or "having been coerced."

2. *Luther's Works*, vol. 4, ed. Jaroslav Pelikan and Helmut T. Lehmann (St. Louis: Concordia, and Philadelphia: Fortress Press, 1955–), p. 357. Cited hereafter as *LW*.

Introduction

1. In Luther's words, "That to which your heart clings and entrusts itself . . . is really your God." See his explanation to the First Commandment in the Large Catechism, *The Book of Concord*, trans. and ed. Theodore G. Tappert (Philadelphia: Fortress Press, 1959), p. 365.

2. See Judith Lewis Herman's brilliant analysis of psychological trauma and the process of healing, *Trauma and Recovery* (New York: Basic Books, 1992).

3. Dorothee Sölle, *Suffering*, trans. Everett R. Kalin (Philadelphia: Fortress, 1975), p. 32.

4. Paul S. Fiddes, *Past Event and Present Salvation: The Christian Idea of Atonement* (Louisville, Ky.: Westminster/

John Knox Press, 1989), p. 180.

5. Douglas John Hall, *Thinking the Faith: Christian Theology in a North American Context* (Minneapolis: Augsburg Publishing House, 1989), p. 35.

6. *Webster's Ninth New Collegiate Dictionary* informs that the word "epistemology" derives from the Greek *episteme*, or knowledge, and provides this definition: "The study or a theory of the nature and grounds of knowledge, especially with reference to its limits and validity."

7. Sandra Harding, *Whose Science? Whose Knowledge? Thinking from Women's Lives* (Ithaca, N.Y.: Cornell University Press, 1991), p. 145.

8. Michael Polanyi, *Personal Knowledge: Towards a Post-Critical Philosophy* (Chicago: University of Chicago Press, 1958, 1962).

9. Richard Rorty, *Philosophy and the Mirror of Nature* (Princeton, N.J.: Princeton University Press, 1979), p. 11.

10. Harding, *Whose Science?*, p. 105.

11. In this dismissal, modern science had ancient precedents, Aristotle among them.

12. See, for example, Elizabeth Kamarck Minnich's work, especially *Transforming Knowledge* (Philadelphia: Temple University Press, 1990); and Sue V. Rosser, *Teaching Science and Health from a Feminist Perspective* (New York: Pergamon Press, 1986).

13. Minnich, *Transforming Knowledge*, p. 160.

14. Relatively little published work addresses Luther's theology from an expressly feminist stance; but see, for example, Elizabeth Bettenhausen's "Dependence, Liberation, and Justification," *Word & World* 7, no. 1 (Winter 1987): 59–69, and Mary D. Pellauer's "Feminist Theology: Challenges and Consolations for Lutherans," *dialog* 24, no. 1 (Winter 1985): 19–25. Other work is doubtless in process.

15. There are many fine books about Luther's theology of the cross. I have relied on several of the best to establish

(in Chapter 2) the intellectual and historical context out of which Luther's own theological contribution emerged. I refer readers to those works, and the works they themselves cite, for treatment of some of the medieval and contemporary philosophers and theologians whose work on, say, justification and the righteousness of God Luther knew and built on. As original and profound as his contribution was, and is, Luther did not make up his theology out of whole cloth, nor—as far as we know—did he transcribe a direct and intelligible revelation from the Holy Spirit. I am *not* delving deeply or broadly into the intellectual "deposit" with which Luther was in conversation—and, often, as it turned out, in deep disagreement; I *am* aware of its significance for Luther's own productions.

16. Douglas John Hall, *Lighten Our Darkness: Toward an Indigenous Theology of the Cross* (Philadelphia: Westminster Press, 1976), p. 164. Much of the scholarship the theology of the cross has inspired depends on a specialized vocabulary accessible mainly to a self-selected and somewhat exclusive theologians' guild. Those who invest the time to learn it may be inclined to challenge the right of the less learned to speak. Those who teach and write Lutheran theology may be especially concerned to guard the terms, vocabulary, and venue of the debate, so that the theology of the cross may continue to make the kind of sense they believe only Luther experts have been able to make of it.

17. What Luther said was probably more intelligible to the sixteenth-century scholars who opposed him bitterly than it could ever be to us. At the same time, the insights Luther sought to disclose to his contemporaries—he was scarcely thinking of *us*!—were grounded in mysteries as elusive and as central to Christian belief then as they had ever been, and as they are today. Gerhard Ebeling points out only one of the many ways Luther's time differed from ours: "Luther lived at a time . . . in which the word 'God' was still understandable without further discussion, and the

claim it implied, together with the right to speak of God, was taken for granted . . . [T]heology itself proceeded . . . from this automatic assumption." See his *Luther: An Introduction to His Thought*, trans. R. A. Wilson (Philadelphia: Fortress Press, 1970), pp. 243–44.

18. Walter Altmann, *Luther and Liberation: A Latin American Perspective*, trans. Mary M. Solberg (Minneapolis: Fortress Press, 1992), p. vii.

19. That we would distinguish "secular" from "religious" is only one clear marker of our historical distance from Luther and his time.

20. Marilyn J. Harran, *Luther on Conversion: The Early Years* (Ithaca, N.Y.: Cornell University Press, 1983), p. 20.

21. Two examples: first, Luther's insistence that knowledge of God and knowledge of humans are inseparably bound up together and relative to each other; and second, his insistence that human access to knowledge of the things of God comes not through the direct contemplation or analysis of them, but rather through a sort of epistemological "back door" involving faith, experience, and "listening" to Scripture.

22. Lorraine Code asks us to "[c]onsider the strangeness a traveler experiences in a country and culture where she has to suspend judgments about the identity and nature of all manner of things from simple artifacts . . . to customs and cultural phenomena," and suggests—correctly, as far as I can see—that "[p]articipation in such situations opens a different perspective on fundamental assumptions that people are accustomed, unthinkingly, to make" (p. 39). See her *What Can She Know? Feminist Theory and the Construction of Knowledge* (Ithaca, N.Y.: Cornell University Press, 1991).

23. To desire to relinquish one's own resistance to knowing of others' suffering, or to standing with them in their suffering, is *very* different from exhorting those who suffer the violence more powerful others impose to accept their suffering.

24. For this phrase I am indebted to Aarne Siirala, who in his *Divine Humanness,* trans. T. A. Kantonen (Philadelphia: Fortress Press, 1970), p. 101, writes of the "cruciform nature of reality."

25. From Walter Brueggemann's "Editor's Foreword" to Charles B. Cousar's *A Theology of the Cross: The Death of Jesus in the Pauline Letters* (Minneapolis: Fortress Press, 1990), p. viii.

26. Ibid.

27. James H. Cone, *God of the Oppressed* (New York: Seabury Press, 1975), p. vi.

Chapter 1

1. Harding, *Whose Science?,* p. 6.

2. A "Roundtable Discussion," edited by Elly Elshout and entitled "Women with Disabilities: A Challenge to Feminist Theology," *Journal of Feminist Studies in Religion* 10, no. 2 (Fall 1994): 99–134, is but one relatively recent instance of how these "wake-up calls" occur.

3. Donna Haraway, one of the feminist theorists whose work informs the following discussion, describes the phenomenon this way: "It has become difficult to name one's feminism by a single adjective—or even to insist in every instance upon the noun. Consciousness of exclusion through naming is acute. Identities seem contradictory, partial, and strategic . . . . [G]ender, race, and class cannot provide the basis for belief in 'essential' unity. There is nothing about being 'female' that naturally binds women . . . . Which identities are available to ground such a potent political myth called 'us', and what could motivate enlistment in this collectivity? Painful fragmentation among feminists (not to mention among women) along every possible fault line has made the concept of *woman* elusive, an excuse for the matrix of women's dominations of each other . . . ." (See

Haraway, *Simians, Cyborgs, and Women: The Reinvention of Nature* [New York: Routledge, 1991], p. 155). Precisely the recognition of what she calls "fractured identities," however, is a necessary component of a constructive, morally persuasive epistemological strategy.

In her "Report from the Bahamas," June Jordan reflects on the ascription of a common identity and on the possible basis for real connection among those with different identities: "I am reaching," she writes, "for the words to describe the difference between a common identity that has been imposed and the individual identity any one of us will choose, once she gains that chance.

"That difference is the one that keeps us stupid in the face of new, specific information about somebody else with whom we are supposed to have a connection because a third party, hostile to both of us, has worked it so that the two of us, like it or not, share a common enemy. *What happens beyond the idea of that enemy and beyond the consequences of that enemy?*

"I am saying that the ultimate connection cannot be the enemy. The ultimate connection must be the need that we find between us. It is not only who you are, in other words, but what we can do for each other that will determine the connection" (p. 47). "Report from the Bahamas" appears in June Jordan's *On Call: Political Essays* (Boston: South End Press, 1985).

4. Minnich, *Transforming Knowledge*, p. 5.

5. I would reiterate here what I suggested at the end of the Introduction, namely, that I am more interested in the general cultural *function* of these "received traditions," and their effect on how we live our lives and what we expect of our institutions and societies, than I am in a critical historical *analysis* of these traditions. It is not offered here; I would argue that for purposes of the proposal I am laying out, such analysis is not necessary, either.

6. Code, *What Can She Know?*, p. ix.

7. Sandra Harding observes that "the history of Western epistemology has been largely a series of responses to various formulations of the problem of skepticism . . . [The] canon . . . is fashioned out of the supposedly fundamental human concern with the problem of whether it is possible for humans to know anything at all." See *Whose Science?*, p. 107.

8. Among other places, Harding refers to this vantage point in "The Instability of Analytical Categories of Feminist Theory," *Signs* 11, no. 4 (1986): 647.

9. In real life, a "value-free fact" is no more interesting—or worthy of consumption—than a "fat-free cheesecake."

10. Code, *What Can She Know?*, p. 35.

11. Haraway, *Simians, Cyborgs, and Women*, p. 111.

12. Code, *What Can She Know?*, p. 1. She also makes this very salutary point, which is often missing from critiques generally: "A recognition that human interests are indeed implicated . . . does not prima facie, invite censure. It does enjoin a sustained moral-political alertness to the need for analysis and critique . . . of the sources out of which claims . . . are made" (p. 48). See also Sandra Harding, *Whose Science?*, p. 149, where she begins her discussion of "strong objectivity" by noting that "our cultures have agendas and make assumptions that we as individuals cannot easily detect," and arguing that these agendas and assumptions ought to be as subject to critical scrutiny as any other evidence mustered to support scientific hypotheses.

13. Elizabeth Kamarck Minnich, "Resisting Reality: Critique and Creativity," *Spotlight on Teaching* 2, no. 2 (1994): 2. This publication is an occasional newspaper published by the American Academy of Religion. Minnich's article is part of an ongoing conversation about her book, *Transforming Knowledge*. The above quotation is a particularly succinct summary of the errors she identifies in the "dominant system of meaning."

14. In the academy, for example, "women's literature" or "black theology" or "feminist philosophy" are subsets of larger disciplines in a quite different sense than "English literature" or "nineteenth-century theology" or "analytic philosophy" are. This becomes clear immediately if one seeks inclusion in the curriculum of "too many" women or black or feminist contributors to their respective fields.

15. Sheila M. Briggs, "The Politics of Identity and the Politics of Interpretation," *Union Seminary Quarterly Review* 43, no. 1 (1989): 165.

16. See Minnich's *Transforming Knowledge*, pp. 95–147, for her examination of a collection of especially potent concepts, each with its own mystifying spin.

17. Ibid., p. 148.

18. Code, *What Can She Know?*, pp. ix–x.

19. In bioethics, see Susan Sherwin's *No Longer Patient: Feminist Ethics and Health Care* (Philadelphia: Temple University Press, 1992), especially pp. 66ff, and Mary B. Mahowald's "On Treatment of Myopia: Feminist Standpoint Theory and Bioethics," in *Feminism & Bioethics: Beyond Reproduction*, ed. Susan Wolf (New York: Oxford University Press, 1996). In theology, see, for example, Ann Kirkus Wetherilt's *That They May Be Many: Voices of Women, Echoes of God* (New York: Continuum, 1994), and Mary McClintock Fulkerson's *Changing the Subject: Women's Discourses and Feminist Theology* (Minneapolis: Fortress Press, 1994).

20. Code, *What Can She Know?*, p. x.

21. Harding, *Whose Science?*, p. 47.

22. Haraway, *Simians, Cyborgs, and Women*, p. 19.

23. Minnich, *Transforming Knowledge*, pp. 32–33.

24. Maria Lugones, "On the Logic of Pluralist Feminism," in *Feminist Ethics*, ed. Claudia Card (Lawrence: University Press of Kansas, 1991), p. 43.

25. Susan Bordo provides a philosophical account of the emergence of Cartesian "objectivism" as "'an aggressive

flight from the 'feminine' rather than (simply) the confident articulation of a positive new epistemological ideal." See her "The Cartesian Masculinization of Thought," in *Signs: Journal of Women in Culture and Society* 11, no. 3 (1986), p. 441.

26. Code, *What Can She Know?*, p. 266.

27. Harding, *Whose Science?*, pp. 109–10.

28. Ibid., p. 132.

29. Minnich, *Transforming Knowledge*, p. 162 (emphasis added).

30. Code, *What Can She Know?*, p. xii. Harding refers to epistemologies that foster "liberatory social relations" (*Whose Science?*, p. xi).

31. Beverly Wildung Harrison, "The Power of Anger in the Work of Love," *Making the Connections: Essays in Feminist Social Ethics*, ed. Carol S. Robb (Boston: Beacon Press, 1985), p. 13. This essay is a classic.

32. Haraway, *Simians, Cyborgs, and Women*, p. 113.

33. Ibid.

34. Briggs, "The Politics of Identity," p. 170.

35. Ibid., p. 171.

36. Ibid., p. 178.

37. Haraway, *Simians, Cyborgs, and Women*, p. 121. Neither Briggs nor Haraway would consider the "fallen-apart-ness" of the world lamentable, nor would either one yearn for the "re-integration" or "restoration" of the world—as if it *had* once been "one" or "not fallen[-apart]."

38. Code, *What Can She Know?*, p. 307.

39. Sharon D. Welch, *Communities of Resistance and Solidarity: A Feminist Theology of Liberation* (Maryknoll, N.Y.: Orbis, 1985), p. ix.

40. Haraway, *Simians, Cyborgs, and Women*, p. 191. Harding concurs: " . . . [T]he view from the perspective of the powerful is far more partial and distorted than that available from the perspective of the dominated; this is so for a variety of reasons. To name just one, the powerful

have far more interests in obscuring the unjust conditions that produce their unearned privileges and authority than do the dominated in hiding the conditions that produce their situation." See *Whose Science?*, p. 59. Both Haraway and Harding express the epistemological privilege of the dominated/subjugated in terms that cannot be separated neatly into "science" and "ethics," though elements of each can be distinguished. Although there is not a trace of theology here—Haraway's reference to the "god-trick" notwithstanding—I judge both these statements to be quite compatible with key dimensions of liberation theologies, especially the "epistemological privilege of the poor."

41. Harding provides a helpful summary of feminist "standpoint" epistemologies in *Whose Science?*, pp. 119ff, in which she makes several key descriptive points about such approaches: (1) They argue that "not just opinions but also a culture's best beliefs—what it calls knowledge—are socially situated" (p. 119); (2) "[t]he distinctive features of women's situation in a gender-stratified society are . . . distinctive resources [for producing] . . . more accurate descriptions and theoretically richer explanations than does conventional research" (p. 119); and (3) " . . . a feminist standpoint is not something that anyone can have simply by claiming it. It is an achievement [and] differs in this respect from a perspective, which anyone can have simply by 'opening one's eyes'" (p. 126). Major feminist standpoint theorists she cites are Nancy Hartsock (see especially her "The Feminist Standpoint: Developing the Ground for a Specifically Feminist Historical Materialism," *Discovering Reality: Feminist Perspectives on Epistemology, Metaphysics, Methodology, and Philosophy of Science*, ed. Sandra Harding and Merrill B. Hintikka [Dordrecht, Holland: D. Reidel, 1983], pp. 283–310; and her *Money, Sex, and Power: Toward a Feminist Historical Materialism* [Boston: Northeastern University Press, 1983]) and Hilary Rose (see "Hand, Brain, and Heart: A Feminist Epistemology for the Natural Sciences," *Signs* 9, no. 1 [1983]). Sara Ruddick

(see especially *Maternal Thinking: Toward a Politics of Peace* [Boston: Beacon Press, 1989]) can also be argued to work from standpoint theory; according to Harding, while Ruddick's arguments do not develop into a standpoint epistemology, they could be used to do so.

42. Harding, *Whose Science?*, p. 275. Patricia Hill Collins, who invented the term "outsider within," is particularly instructive on this standpoint in "Learning from the Outsider Within: The Sociological Significance of Black Feminist Thought," *Social Problems* 33, no. 6 (1986). See also her *Black Feminist Thought: Knowledge, Consciousness, and the Politics of Empowerment* (New York: Routledge, 1991).

43. bell hooks, "Choosing the Margin as a Place of Radical Openness," in *Yearning: Race, Gender, and Cultural Politics*, ed. bell hooks (Boston: South End Press, 1990), p. 150.

44. Code, *What Can She Know?*, pp. 307–308.

45. June Jordan treats "identity politics" with great insight. In "Report from the Bahamas," (Chapter 6 in her book *On Call: Political Essays*) she ruminates about race, class, and gender as she spends her vacation in a multinational hotel on the beach and her tourist dollars at the local crafts market. "Yes," she writes, "race and class and gender remain as real as the weather. But what they must mean about the contact between two individuals is less obvious and, like the weather, not predictable. . . . They may serve well as indicators of commonly felt conflict, but as elements of connection they seem about as reliable as precipitation probability for the day after the night before the day" (p. 46). The essay is a gem.

46. Code, *What Can She Know?*, p. xi.

47. Harding, *Whose Science?*, p. 159.

48. In this connection, see *A Mind of One's Own: Essays on Reason and Objectivity*, eds. Louise M. Antony and Charlotte Witt (New York: Westview Press, 1994), a collection of essays by women in philosophy who, responsive to

other feminists' attacks on reason and objectivity as patriarchal, and fundamentally flawed, philosophical norms, argue that "traditional" philosophical methods and texts (from Aristotle through Quine) still have much to contribute to feminism. Their project, insofar as it involves looking in a new way at some of the great old men of the (philosophical) tradition and with a rephrased if not entirely new agenda, bears some interesting resemblances to the project unfolding in this book.

49. Philosopher Lisa Heldke rightly has reminded me that feminists are often very critical of postmodernism's relativism, which (they argue) has emerged at a time at which disenfranchised people are making truth claims about what is right and wrong. Just when the previously excluded appeal to categories like reason, truth, and objectivity, someone comes along and says, "Oh, it's all relative." See also Harding's comments below about the historical emergence of the concept of relativism in Europe.

50. Evelyn Fox Keller explores (among other things) how and why objectivism has been associated with domination, particularly male domination. Her discussion, which draws on psychoanalytic theory (especially object relations), is both fascinating and salutary. See her *Reflections on Gender and Science* (New Haven, Conn.: Yale University Press, 1985).

51. "The view from nowhere," a phrase generally associated with philosopher Thomas Nagel, is the title of his 1986 book (New York: Oxford University Press).

52. Harding, *Whose Science?*, p. 97.

53. Code, *What Can She Know?*, p. 2.

54. Haraway, *Simians, Cyborgs, and Women*, p. 191.

55. Harding, *Whose Science?*, p. 155.

56. Haraway, *Simians, Cyborgs, and Women*, p. 187.

57. Ibid.

58. Harding, *Whose Science?*, pp. 147, 149.

59. Ibid., p. 285.

60. Note that "partiality" has a different ring here than

it did in Minnich's description of "partial knowledge." Here, "partial" refers self-consciously and unapologetically to the character of knowledge of whatever sort or subject. Most feminist epistemological reflection also values "partiality" (in the sense of "partisanship") toward the knowledge of those who are marginalized by the dominant and "partiality" toward their welfare. As long as the meaning and import of the terms are clarified, there is no problem in using them in a variety of ways.

61. Haraway, *Simians, Cyborgs, and Women,* p. 193.

62. Ibid., p. 198.

63. Keller's notion of "dynamic objectivity" further illustrates and illuminates feminists' contributions to epistemology. " . . . [D]ynamic objectivity," she writes, "is not unlike empathy, a form of knowledge of other persons that draws explicitly on the commonality of feelings and experience in order to enrich one's understanding of another in his or her own right . . . . [At the same time] it recognizes difference between self and other as an opportunity for a deeper and more articulated kinship." Ideally, Keller observes, a scientist's attention to the natural world, informed by this notion of objectivity, is "a form of love" (Keller, *Reflections on Gender and Science,* p. 117).

64. Haraway, *Simians, Cyborgs, and Women,* p. 201.

65. Minnich, *Transforming Knowledge,* p. 32. Emphasis in the original.

66. While the ethical dimensions of knowledge concern men as well as women, feminist thinkers have insisted more urgently than men that they be responded to. Alison M. Jaggar's observation about feminist ethics would apply equally to feminist epistemologies: " . . . [I]t would be a mistake to identify feminist ethics with attention to some explicitly gendered subset of ethical issues. On the contrary, rather than being limited to a restricted ethical domain, feminist ethics has *enlarged* the traditional concern of ethics. Approaching social life with an explicitly feminist conscious-

ness has enabled it both to identify previously unrecognized ethical issues and to introduce fresh perspectives on issues already acknowledged as having an ethical dimension." See her essay, "Feminist Ethics: Projects, Problems, Prospects," *Feminist Ethics*, ed. Claudia Card (Lawrence: University Press of Kansas, 1991), p. 86.

67. Minnich, focusing on a slightly larger field of vision, observes, "[T]hat all these systems also, and profoundly, damage in some ways those who benefit from them can be recognized without thereby excusing them/us from responsibility for their perpetuation" (Minnich, *Transforming Knowledge*, p. 33).

68. Code, *What Can She Know?*, p. 72.

69. Margaret Urban Walker, "Moral Understandings: Alternative 'Epistemology' for Feminist Ethics," *Explorations in Feminist Ethics: Theory and Practice*, eds. Eve Browning Cole and Susan Coultrap-McQuin (Bloomington: Indiana University Press, 1982), p. 166 (emphasis added).

70. Code, *What Can She Know?*, p. 38.

71. Margaret Urban Walker, "Moral Understandings," p. 167.

Chapter 2

1. According to Joseph E. Vercruysse, Luther himself used the expressions *theologia crucis* and *theologus crucis* (theologian of the cross) in only five texts: "Four of them were written in the spring of 1518, namely the *Asterisci Lutheri adversus Obeliscos Eckii*, the *Lectures on Hebrews*, the *Resolutiones disputationum de indulgentiarum virtute* and finally the famous Heidelberg Disputation. The fifth one is in the *Operationes in Psalmos*, Luther's second course on the Psalms, held from 1519 to 1521." The first four were probably written between February and April 1518, just

before the meeting in Heidelberg. See Vercruysse, "Luther's Theology of the Cross at the Time of the Heidelberg Disputation," *Gregorianum* 57 (1976): 532–48.

2. *LW,* vol. 31, pp. 40–41. Please note that while I have used inclusive language in writing this book, quoted material appears as I found it.

In *Luther's Theology of the Cross* (Oxford: Basil Blackwell, 1985)—one of the finest available expositions of the emergence of Luther's *theologia crucis* out of and in contrast to the theology of his time—Alister McGrath offers his own translation of Theses 19 and 20, as follows:

19. The man who looks upon the invisible things of God as they are perceived in created things does not deserve to be called a theologian. (*Non ille dignus theologus dicitur, qui invisibilia Dei per ea, quae facta sunt, intellecta conspicit.*)

20. The man who perceives the visible rearward parts of God as seen in suffering and the cross does, however, deserve to be called a theologian. (*Sed qui visibilia et posteriora Dei per passiones et crucem conspecta intelligit.*)

McGrath comments that the translation in Thesis 20 of *posteriora Dei* as "the manifest things of God" is "clearly unacceptable. Not only is the important allusion to Exodus 33.23 overlooked: on the basis of this translation, it is impossible to speak of the *hiddenness* of God's revelation—yet it is clear that this is precisely what Luther intended to convey by the phrase" (p. 48). McGrath's point is well taken.

Another translation of these two theses, this one by James Atkinson, provides a few more nuances:

19. He is not worth calling a theologian who seeks to interpret "the invisible things of God"

on the basis of the things which have been created.

20. But he is worth calling a theologian who understands the visible and hinder parts of God to mean the passion and the cross.

See *Luther: Early Theological Works*, vol. 16, Library of Christian Classics, ed. and trans. James Atkinson (Philadelphia: Westminster Press, 1962), p. 278.

3. Martin Brecht, *Martin Luther: His Road to Reformation 1483–1521*, trans. James L. Schaaf (Philadelphia: Fortress Press, 1985), p. 175.

4. Ebeling, *Luther: An Introduction,* p. 32.

5. The first part of the quotation—"Experience . . . theologian"—is from *LW,* vol. 54, p. 7 (part of the famous Table Talk compendium); the second part—"It is by living . . . or speculating"—is found in *D. Martin Luthers Werke: Kritische Gesamtausgabe* (Weimar: Hermann Böhlaus Nachfolger, 1883–) 5, 163, 28. Cited hereafter as *WA.* The combination of the two quotes seems both fair and mutually illuminating.

6. Ebeling, *Luther: An Introduction,* p. 33. Ebeling also observes that "[f]or Luther, theology as the object of intellectual inquiry and theology as the sphere of a personal encounter, formed an indivisible unity" (pp. 95–96).

7. Owen Chadwick, *The Reformation* (New York: Penguin Books, 1964, 1972), p. 11.

8. Altmann, *Luther and Liberation,* pp. 2–3.

9. For a discussion of the importance for Luther of humanist scholars' activity in reviving the study of biblical languages, and the significance of Luther's knowledge and use of Hebrew, see McGrath, *Luther's Theology of the Cross,* especially pp. 40–53 and 100–102.

10. Brecht, *Road to Reformation,* pp. 130–131.

11. Ebeling, *Luther: An Introduction,* pp. 70–71.

12. Brecht, *Road to Reformation,* p. 132.

13. McGrath, *Luther's Theology of the Cross,* pp. 8–9.

14. John Dillenberger, like many Luther scholars, re-counts the dramatic story of Luther's being caught in a violent thunderstorm during which he was struck by a bolt of lightning that nearly killed him. Luther cried out to St. Anne, the patron saint of miners (he had spent his youth in the heart of the mining district of Thuringia), "Help! I will become a monk!" and two weeks thereafter, entered the Augustinian cloister in Erfurt. Dillenberger speculates that, "[w]hile the thunderstorm precipitated the decision to become a monk, the possibility of that course of action was surely part and parcel of Luther's natural and educational equipment." See John Dillenberger, introduction to *Martin Luther: Selections from His Writings,* ed. John Dillenberger (Garden City, N.Y.: Anchor Books, 1961), p. xv.

15. See, for example, Erik H. Erikson's *Young Man Luther: A Study in Psychoanalysis and History* (New York: W. W. Norton, 1958), a theologically and spiritually fascinating psychoanalytic study of Luther's development as a man and as a theologian. Erikson by no means reduces Luther's theological insights to resolutions of his internal childhood conflicts about and with his father, as some Luther hagiographers claim.

16. William Hordern, *Experience and Faith: The Significance of Luther for Understanding Today's Experiential Religion* (Minneapolis: Augsburg Publishing House, 1983), p. 52.

17. Harran notes that Luther transformed Augustine's view of the human being as *curvatus,* or turned toward the lesser good, into *incurvatus in se ipsum,* surely a stronger denial of any human capacity to approach God. (See Harran, *Luther on Conversion,* p. 101.) Dillenberger points out that Luther's notion of the "bondage of the will," elucidated most forcefully in Luther's 1519 treatise of the same name (see *LW,* vol. 33), written in response to Erasmus, underscores the same point, namely, "that there is no act or

capacity of will by which the self can successfully will itself into an adequate and proper relation to God" (Dillenberger, *Martin Luther: Selections,* p. xxvii). What earlier generations called man's [sic] "total depravity" was a concept Luther used to challenge scholastic theology's optimism with regard to the capacity of natural human reason to establish the basis for receiving revelation. For Luther the notion of total depravity referred to the pervasive corruption and disorientation that characterizes every aspect of human life (every aspect of which, it must be noted, is in relation to God as the creature's Creator and Sustainer). Human reason, as self-interested as any other human faculty, "thinks up" or "speculates" the sort of God that suits it (see Hordern, *Experience and Faith,* pp. 65ff.).

18. McGrath, *Luther's Theology of the Cross,* p. 110.

19. In the explanations to the theses of the Heidelberg disputation, Luther laid out the dilemma: "Man either knows whether he does what is in him, or he does not know it. If he knows it, then he knows that he has grace, since they say that grace is certainly given to him who does what is in him. If he does not know it, this doctrine is erroneous and his consolation ceases. For whatever work he has done, he does not know whether he has done what is in him. Consequently he always remains in doubt" (*LW,* vol. 31, p. 67).

20. Quoted as translated by McGrath, *Luther's Theology of the Cross,* pp. 96–97. See also *LW,* vol. 34, pp. 336–7. Paul's passionate and convinced student, Luther credited the apostle with directing him, theologically and spiritually, (back?) to Christ. "What others have learned from Scholastic theology is their own affair," Luther wrote in 1545. "As for me, I . . . certainly did not learn there what the power of God is, and the work of God, the grace of God, the righteousness of God. . . . Indeed, I lost Christ there, but now I have found him again in Paul" (quoted in *Luther: Lectures on Romans,* ed. Wilhelm Pauck [Philadelphia: Westminster Press, 1961], pp. xxxix–xl; see *WA* 12, 414, 22). Luther's

words here—"I lost Christ there [in scholastic theology]"—expresses with characteristic dramatic flair, and seriousness, his heartfelt rejection of the tradition in which he had been so thoroughly schooled.

21. McGrath, *Luther's Theology of the Cross,* p. 92.

22. Harran proposes an equivalence between "how a person comes to be justified before God" and "how a person is converted to God." Luther himself, she writes, experienced "a long process of discovery and conversion . . . in which [he] came to perceive how God converts man—without his aid, indeed even without his arriving at a passively receptive state of humility." Conversion, Harran continues, "means not only the acceptance of Christ and of divine wisdom but the rejection of one's own plan for attaining salvation based on human knowledge" (Harran, *Luther on Conversion,* pp. 20, 68).

23. On Luther's knowledge of Hebrew and the "semantic suggestion" of another kind of *iustitia Dei* contained in *sdqh,* the Hebrew term translated in the Septuagint as *iustitia,* see McGrath, *Luther's Theology of the Cross,* p. 100ff.

24. Ibid., p. 133.

25. " . . . for one is at the same time both a sinner and a righteous person: a sinner in fact, but righteous by the sure imputation and promise of God that He will continue to deliver the believer from sin until He has completely cured him. . . ." (*LW,* vol. 25, p. 260).

26. McGrath, *Luther's Theology of the Cross,* p. 154 (emphasis added).

27. *LW,* vol. 31, p. 51.

28. Ebeling, *Luther: An Introduction,* p. 258.

29. Paul Althaus, *The Theology of Martin Luther,* trans. Robert C. Schultz (Philadelphia: Fortress Press, 1966), p. 30.

30. Walther von Loewenich, *Luther's Theology of the Cross,* trans. Herbert J. A. Bouman (Belfast: Christian Journals Limited, 1976), p. 18.

31. McGrath, *Luther's Theology of the Cross,* p. 1.

32. *WA* 5, 176, 32–33.

33. von Loewenich does a very illuminating "brief overview in chronological order on the definitions of the concept 'theology of the cross' in the past literature"—covering the years 1862 (A. Harnack) through 1927 (E. Wolf)—in the Notes section of his book, *Luther's Theology of the Cross,* pp. 169–73. See also McGrath's comment that "the first serious studies of Luther's *theologia crucis* date from the period immediately after [the First World War]" (McGrath, *Luther's Theology of the Cross,* p. 179).

34. von Loewenich, in discussing the "understanding of faith" as it "belongs within the realm of Luther's theology of the cross," makes the following observation:

> [F]aith maintains itself in man's reality. It is not only the negation of human possibility, but its realization as well. Faith leads to knowledge. But . . . the faith character of this realization dare never be overlooked. That means, this 'being realized' cannot be made the starting point of a self-contained system. For as surely as one must in all statements constantly reckon with revelation whose correlate is faith, so little may one 'reckon' with it, because in that way it would be deprived of its epochal character . . . .[I]t is not the understanding as such, but only the understanding of faith that proves itself as faith's vehicle of knowledge (von Loewenich, *Luther's Theology of the Cross,* pp. 64–65).

If von Loewenich is right about how the understanding of faith works for Luther's theology—and I believe he is right—he may also be read to be explaining several other things, among them, why Luther never produced, and probably never seriously considered producing, a *systematic* theology; why it makes more sense to treat the theology of the cross as an "approach" or method, rather than as a "theology" per se; why later Lutheran legalists, with their bloodless passion for establishing what Luther *really* meant, often found themselves trapped within their own self-constructed, "self-contained system[s]."

35. McGrath's *Luther's Theology of the Cross* provides a particularly clear account, which involves great intellectual appreciation for Luther's roots in medieval and contemporary (fifteenth- and sixteenth-century) thought.

36. See Luther's Preface to the New Testament (1522) and his Preface to the Epistle of St. Paul to the Romans (1522), in which he indicates where he believes Christ is found most clearly in his translations of these texts. From the former: "The true kernel and marrow of all the books [of the New Testament] . . . are the gospel of John and St. Paul's epistles, especially that to the Romans . . . " (quoted in Dillenberger, *Martin Luther: Selections,* p. 18). From the latter: "This epistle is in truth the most important document in the New Testament, the gospel in its purest expression . . . . It is the soul's daily bread, and can never be read too often, or studied too much . . . [I]t is a brilliant light, almost enough to illumine the whole Bible" (quoted in Dillenberger, *Martin Luther: Selections,* p. 19).

37. Jon Sobrino elucidates the contrast between "the principle of analogical knowledge" and "the principle of dialectical knowledge: i.e., knowing something means knowing it through its contrary. If God is really present in the cross of Jesus, then he is there first and foremost as someone contradicting the world and all that we consider to be true and good. God appears on the cross *sub specie contrarii* . . . . The very first consequence of Jesus' cross for Christians is a complete break with their customary epistemology. The cross shatters the self-interest that motivates us to gain knowledge of the deity. The cross breaks the inertia of analogical thinking and transforms it into dialectical

thinking." See Sobrino's *Christology at the Crossroads: A Latin American Approach*, trans. John Drury (Maryknoll, N.Y.: Orbis Books, 1978), pp. 198–9.

38. McGrath, *Luther's Theology of the Cross,* p. 160.

39. *LW,* vol. 10.

40. *LW,* vol. 11 (see also the explanations of the Heidelberg disputation, specifically Thesis 20, at *LW,* vol. 31, p. 52).

41. The Pauline text (I Cor. 1:26–2:13) articulates this paradoxical truth repeatedly, referring, for example, to the believers to whom Paul is writing, to God's work itself, to Paul's message and his demeanor, and to what the world understands.

42. McGrath, *Luther's Theology of the Cross,* p. 167.

43. Brian Gerrish observes that Luther faults reason "at two points: first, although it believes that God *can* aid, it does not believe that God *will* do so *for it*; second, though it knows *that* God is, it does not know *who* or *what* God is ... [, that is,] ... reason attaches its notions of Deity to the wrong object, that is, not to the God who reveals Himself in Christ ...." See his *Grace and Reason: A Study in the Theology of Luther* (Oxford: At the Clarendon Press, 1962), p. 15.

44. Hall, *Lighten Our Darkness,* p. 120.

45. Ebeling, *Luther: An Introduction,* p. 256.

46. Vercruysse makes a point of the subtle but crucial significance of Luther's focusing on the *theologian* of the cross, rather than on the *theology* of the cross. "Luther," he says, "is more interested in the existential attitude of the theologian than in developing a theology of the cross." Given Luther's own intense wrestling with his relation with God, and his lifelong commitment to articulating the practical as well as the theological implications of what he believed the gospel revealed about God's promise of grace to sinners, this focus on the theologizing person is not surprising. After all, Vercruysse continues, Luther knew that

"[t]he theologian of the cross is the sinner, the evildoer, the fool and weakling, the needy and poor man. He experiences God's love, which creates out of nothing what deserves love and makes . . . the needy sinner righteous, good, wise, strong." The true theologian of the cross, Luther would have said, is the one who apprehends all this—in faith. (See Vercruysse, "Luther's Theology," p. 539.)

47. *LW,* vol. 31, pp. 52–53.

48. Perhaps most uncompromisingly in Bondage of the Will (*LW,* vol. 33), which Luther considered his best work, one of few he thought should survive him.

49. In his Disputation Against Scholastic Theology (1517) Luther asserted, "Man is by nature unable to want God to be God. Indeed, he himself wants to be God and does not want God to be God" (*LW,* vol. 31, p. 10). For Luther this is the kernel of human nature *coram Deo*—which is where humans always are, whether they recognize it or not. Luther, again: "Man's being in the sight of God defines the meaning of his being in the world, whether he admits this or not" (Bondage of the Will, *LW,* vol. 33).

50. *LW,* vol. 31, p. 53.

51. Paul L. Lehmann argues that Luther interpreted the Decalogue descriptively rather than prescriptively: "For Luther . . . the Commandments are not *prescriptive* statements of duties toward God and one's neighbor in a world that God has created, redeemed, and will make new. They are, on the contrary, *descriptive* statements of what happens behaviorally in a world that God has made for being human in—given, in Jesus Christ, a second chance . . . —and promises to bring to . . . fullness . . . in a new heaven and a new earth." See Lehmann's posthumously published *The Decalogue and a Human Future: The Meaning of the Commandments for Making and Keeping Human Life Human* (Grand Rapids, Mich.: William B. Eerdmans Publishing, 1995), p. 22.

52. *LW,* vol. 31, p. 53.

53. Fiddes, *Past Event,* p. 32.

54. *LW,* vol. 33, p. 62.

55. *WA* 10¹˒¹, 527, 11ff, Postil for Epiphany, on Isaiah 60:1–6, quoted by Gerrish in *Grace and Reason,* p. 12.

56. Christopher Morse characterizes Luther's view of the relation of faith and reason in this way: "As long as one does not know the Christ crucified of the gospel one does not know the character of the reality in which all creatures live and move and have their being . . . . This is not an argument . . . of faith versus reason. The disagreement [with scholastics schooled in Aristotle] has to do with the capacity to recognize the premises of reasoning intrinsic to faith. What is rejected is . . . that a logic which is universally demonstrable with respect to things as they presently appear in this world can lead one to a true recognition of ultimate reality." See his *Not Every Spirit: A Dogmatics of Christian Disbelief* (Valley Forge, Penn.: Trinity Press International, 1994), p. 22.

57. Gerrish, *Grace and Reason,* p. 103.

58. von Loewenich, *Luther's Theology of the Cross,* p. 69. See *LW,* vol. 25, pp. 362ff.

59. In his lectures on Romans, Luther wrote: "If the word of God comes, it comes contrary to our thinking and our will. It does not allow our thinking to stand, even in those matters which are most sacred, but it destroys and eradicates and scatters everything . . . " (*LW,* vol. 25, p. 415).

60. *LW,* vol. 25, p. 411.

61. *LW,* vol. 31, p. 53.

62. Althaus, *Theology,* p. 190.

63. Hordern, *Experience and Faith,* p. 90. Hordern's eloquent description of Luther's emphasis on Jesus' humanity underscores what I have called the "epistemological" sense in which the cross reverses human expectations: "Where the human expectation is that God will appear with supernatural and miraculous evidence, in Jesus God comes as a child born in a lowly manger and nursed at Mary's

breast. God does not appear as a king, a person of authority, or a brilliant scholar. God comes as a lowly carpenter who sees the idea of ruling over others as a temptation of the devil . . . . Jesus had a brief period of popularity, but he was soon deserted by the crowds and . . . even his disciples. He died the most despicable and humiliating death that the Romans could invent" (p. 88).

64. Ebeling explains that Luther understands "conscience" as "the sense that [one] is always, and not merely in some particular respect but in [one's] very person, claimed, commanded, questioned, and subjected to judgement, so that in one way or another [one] is always a determined, listening and receiving conscience; either confused or arrogant in an imaginary freedom, which means . . . bondage to the powers of this world; or assured and comforted in obedient attention to God, which is true freedom with regard to the world" (Ebeling, *Luther: An Introduction,* p. 261).

65. Fiddes, *Past Event,* pp. 193, 179.

66. Hall, *Thinking the Faith* pp. 25, 27. " . . . [T]he theology of the cross, at base, is about *God's abiding commitment to the world"* (p. 25). Hall observes that this divine commitment to the world, which is central to classical Hebraic thought (the "pathos of Yahweh"), is the "matrix for our contemplation of the meaning of the cross" (p. 27). Luther's insight that the "righteousness of God" is (from the human creature's point of view) a *salvific* righteousness rooted in the Hebrew notion of *tsedeqah,* lends credence to Hall's observation. (See McGrath, *Luther's Theology of the Cross,* pp. 47–48 and pp. 100–101.)

67. One might say that Luther experienced what feminists call "lived contradiction," a clear sense that the widely, even generally, accepted "wisdom" about something runs counter to one's own sense of what is the case, a sense gleaned from having run up against this conflict in one's own life experience.

68. Althaus, *Theology,* p. 8.

69. *LW,* vol. 21, p. 299. In this particular context, Luther makes the point that "the Blessed Virgin Mary is speaking [this sacred hymn of praise] on the basis of her own experience, in which she was enlightened and instructed by the Holy Spirit."

70. Hordern, *Experience and Faith,* p. 98.

71. von Loewenich, *Luther's Theology of the Cross,* p. 94.

72. Althaus observes that Luther's reliance on both Scripture and experience to explain the human condition is not a contradiction. "[T]he words of Scripture, at least the confessions of the psalmists and of the Apostle Paul . . . describe the experiences of the writers when they were encountered by God. Thus Luther's appeal to Scripture is at the same time an appeal to men's experience of their relationship to God" (Althaus, *Theology,* p. 142). Aarne Siirala observes that "The Bible became authoritative for [Luther], because through it his life and experience took on new meaning and value . . . . The sacred writings convinced him that his human experience had contained a confrontation with the divine and that in his dialogue with life he had listened to a divine word" (Siirala, *Divine Humanness,* p. 38).

73. Hall, *Lighten Our Darkness,* p. 119.

74. Ibid., p. 120.

75. There is no easy translation for the German word *Anfechtung;* because it is central in Luther's life and theological expression, it has become a quite controverted term in theological circles. Margaret R. Miles says it may be understood as an existential state between despair and faith, "a highly intensified and concentrated experience of unbearable tension." See page 243 of her article "'The Rope Breaks When It Is Tightest': Luther on the Body, Consciousness, and the Word," *Harvard Theological Review* 77, nos. 3–4 (1984): 239–58. McGrath says "[it] is not some form of

spiritual growing pains, which . . . disappear when a mystical puberty is attained, but a perennial and authentic feature of the Christian life . . . , [T]he Christian . . . must continually be forced back to the foot of the cross . . . —and this takes place through the continued experience of *Anfechtung*" (McGrath, *Luther's Theology of the Cross,* p. 171). Cassell's German-English, English-German dictionary gives "temptation" as its theological definition. Joseph Sittler's observation about Luther may define it best: "Time and again in his own confessions, Luther talks about moments of what he calls *Anfechtungen,* when he had the horrible fear that he might have been wrong." See Sittler's *Gravity and Grace: Reflections and Provocations,* ed. Linda-Marie Delloff (Minneapolis: Augsburg Publishing House, 1986), p. 24.

76. Ebeling, *Luther: An Introduction,* p. 265.

77. Hall, *Lighten Our Darkness,* p. 123. See also Ebeling's comment that "the emphasis [in what Luther says about God] is not on flight *from* need, but on a refuge *in* need, not upon a change in circumstances, but on a changed attitude to the circumstances . . . " (p. 255).

78. Sittler observes that "equipment" means more than "that which we need to do the thing we want or ought or are called to do. . . . Equipment—*katartismos* in Greek—is also used to mean an internal nurture, an internal formation that matures one's competence for an appointed task," and quotes Hebrews 13:20–21: "Now may the God of peace who brought again from the dead our Lord Jesus . . . equip you with everything good that you may do his will . . . " (Sittler, *Gravity and Grace,* pp. 29–30).

79. Ebeling, *Luther: An Introduction,* p. 228.

80. von Loewenich, *Luther's Theology of the Cross,* p. 112.

81. Althaus, *Theology,* p. 27.

82. Vercruysse contends that in contrasting a theology of glory and a theology of the cross, "it seems that describing the *consequences for a man's life* [of a theology of glory]

is more important to Luther than developing the theological foundation . . . ." Furthermore, "Luther is more interested in the *existential attitude of the theologian* [of the cross] than in developing a theology of the cross." See Vercruysse, "Luther's Theology," pp. 537, 539 (emphasis added).

83. von Loewenich, *Luther's Theology of the Cross,* p. 112.

84. Ebeling, *Luther: An Introduction,* p. 176.

85. Hall, *Lighten Our Darkness,* p. 117 (emphasis added).

86. von Loewenich, *Luther's Theology of the Cross,* p. 53.

87. Ibid., p. 82.

88. *LW,* vol. 36, p. 69.

89. von Loewenich, *Luther's Theology of the Cross,* p. 123.

90. Altmann observes, "Although Luther never stopped proclaiming justification by faith in his writings and in innumerable sermons, he was very sparing—especially in his sermons—in describing his personal experience. He did not use his own experience of justification to persuade others to attempt to have the same experience . . . . [T]his would have represented the denial of justification by grace . . . . [For Luther the] personal experience is necessary and profound, but it is also particular and nontransferable. Luther's testimony is never 'personal'; for Luther this is clearly not what is important. What is important is the objective reality of justification in Christ" (Altmann, *Luther and Liberation,* p. 33).

91. *LW,* vol. 31, p. 53.

92. Ibid.

93. Ibid.

94. Ibid.

95. Among expositions of Luther's doctrine of faith, von Loewenich's may well be the clearest and most careful. The brief discussion that follows here, while it touches on

only a few aspects of Luther's view of faith that will bear on the arguments made later in this book, seeks to keep von Loewenich's nuanced appreciation of Luther's doctrine in mind. See his *Luther's Theology of the Cross*, pp. 50–111.

96. Althaus, *Theology*, p. 43.

97. From Luther's lectures on Hebrews, in *WA* 68, 27f, quoted by Vercruysse, "Luther's Theology," p. 530.

98. Paul Althaus, *The Ethics of Martin Luther*, trans. Robert C. Schultz (Philadelphia: Fortress Press, 1972), p. 17.

99. Luther identifies the ear, rather than the eye, as the "most direct access to the 'bottom of the heart'," writes Miles. "Ideally, Luther says, the Scriptures should not have been written . . . . The function of preaching is [to translate] . . . the written word of Scripture into the living Word which transforms the existential situation of the hearer into the presence of God, a confrontation that questions, convicts, and redeems" (Miles, "The Rope Breaks," pp. 248, 249).

100. Althaus, *Theology*, p. 231.

101. von Loewenich, *Luther's Theology of the Cross*, pp. 84–85.

102. *LW*, vol. 35, pp. 370–71, quoted in Althaus, *Ethics*, pp. 13–14.

Chapter 3

1. Grace Jantzen has made some very helpful observations about this phenomenon, including this one: " . . . [T]he experience itself as well as the response to it occurs within a framework . . . . Nevertheless, the experience can lead one to reconsider the available alternatives. . . . And this reciprocity . . . is part of the basic pattern of rationality, in which questioning occurs from within a perspective, but in which the answers obtained by that questioning can in turn modify that perspective, sometimes radically, leading to

deepening understanding and thus to a new round of questioning." See her "Epistemology, Religious Experience, and Religious Belief," *Modern Theology* 3, no. 4 (1987): 289.

2. von Loewenich, *Luther's Theology of the Cross*, p. 20.

3. From a theological point of view, this relationship is definitively, even constitutively, conditioned by the fact that humans are sinners and God redeems sinners.

4. See also John R. Loeschen, *Wrestling with Luther: An Introduction to the Study of His Thought* (St. Louis, Mo.: Concordia Publishing House, 1976), in which Loeschen makes a very good case for the notion that God is epistemologically *pro nobis*.

5. Any more, one might add, than knowledge is generated by epistemology.

6. Althaus, *Theology*, p. 8.

7. Hall, *Thinking the Faith*, p. 370.

8. Ibid., p. 371.

9. Ibid., p. 382.

10. Ibid., pp. 384, 387.

11. Code, *What Can She Know?*, p. 165.

12. Hall, *Thinking the Faith*, p. 401. Two niggling caveats are in order: Hall does not acknowledge the credit feminist epistemologies deserve; since he does not seem to have read their work, he may also be taking the "new modesty" of "worldly reason" more seriously and appreciatively than it deserves to be taken.

13. These observations in Chung Hyun Kyung's *Struggle to Be the Sun Again: Introducing Asian Women's Theology* (Maryknoll, N.Y.: Orbis Books, 1990) make it clear that others, too, struggle with the question of the responsibility of privileged theologians: "Many educated women theologians in Asia know that they are not doing theology *for* the poor women. They articulate theology in order to enhance the liberation process . . . . These women do theology as a form of repentance and self-criticism. They also do theology

in order to become more critically aware of their privilege and their responsibility in relation to the poor women in their communities . . . . [They] know that this process of *metanoia* to poor women is the only way to regain their wholeness" (p. 102).

14. A comment Haraway makes about the European tradition of binary analysis is apt here: "Noting this tradition does not invalidate its use; it *locates* its use and insists on its partiality and accountability" (Haraway, *Simians, Cyborgs, and Women,* p. 111).

15. Ibid., p. 188.

16. While neither Chapter 1 on feminist epistemologies nor Chapter 2 on Luther's theology of the cross had a separate section on power, the subject threaded its way through both chapters; this section draws on those discussions and makes the matter explicit.

17. Harding, "The Instability of Analytical Categories," p. 647.

18. According to Hall, "A theology of the cross is not a theology of answers; it is a theology of the question" (Hall, *Lighten Our Darkness,* p. 203).

19. Haraway, *Simians, Cyborgs, and Women,* p. 157.

20. It is not, according to any self-respecting interpretation of "revelation," the *source* of all knowing.

21. Chung, *Struggle to Be the Sun,* p. 104.

22. Harding, *Whose Science?,* p. 311.

23. Hall, *Lighten Our Darkness,* p. 121. There is a strong suggestion here that if there is any "glory" in the cross and the suffering it causes and represents, it derives from the solidarity God demonstrates in choosing to join the human experience utterly and without reservation, even to death on a cross. Neither Jesus the man, nor Jesus the One God raised, *invented* the cross, an instrument of torture and death long before Jesus' experience of and association with it.

24. Ibid., p. 116.

25. Haraway, *Simians, Cyborgs, and Women,* p. 192.

26. William Rankin, "The Moral Use of Knowledge: Part 2," *Plumbline* 11, no. 1 (April 1983): 10–11.

27. See, for example, Jon Sobrino, *The True Church and the Poor*, trans. Matthew J. O'Connell (Maryknoll, N.Y.: Orbis Books, 1984), pp. 24ff.

28. Tomás Hanks, in his article "El testimonio evangélico a los pobres y opimidos" (*Vida y Pensamiento* 4, nos. 1–2, 1984), observes that Latin American theologian Hugo Assmann was apparently the first one to speak of the "epistemological privilege of the poor" (p. 40). Assmann's discussion can be found in *Theology in the Americas*, ed. Sergio Torres and John Eagleson (Maryknoll, N.Y.: Orbis Books, 1976), especially pp. 299–300: ". . . [W]hat about the epistemological privilege of the poor? . . . In what sense can we say that these poor and oppressed people who have the internalized oppressor within themselves are privileged to hear the word of God better than the rich ones? . . . The privileged poor of the gospel are the struggling poor, struggling within a holistic perspective of revolution" (p. 300).

29. During my tenure in El Salvador, I was always thunderstruck when, after a group of U.S. visitors had spent a couple of hours listening to the stories of the Mothers of the Disappeared or to officials of the nongovernmental Human Rights Commission, at least one earnest soul would take me aside to ask whether "we're going to get a chance to hear the other side of the story."

30. Jon Sobrino and Juan Hernández Pico, *Theology of Christian Solidarity*, p. 11. I have taken the liberty of changing third-person to first-person plural pronouns. I am confident Sobrino would not mind. Sobrino's insistence, in *Christology at the Crossroads*, that the cross must produce "a crisis for all knowledge of God" is a theological illumination of how this sort of epistemological reversal occurs. Is Jesus' cross truly a scandal, Sobrino asks, if in the face of real human crucifixions we are able to objectify it as a "noetic mystery," which "supposedly can be explained in terms of

God's design and its salvific value for human beings" (p. 187)? Like his or her predecessors, a late-twentieth-century person who searches for God by following Jesus to the cross discovers there not satisfying answers but unnerving questions, among them, What is your interest in being here? and What sort of God did you expect to find, anyway? Logic is stood on its head.

31. Fiddes, *Past Event,* p. 200.

32. Harding, *Whose Science?,* pp. 271, 295, 271.

33. hooks, "Choosing the Margin," pp. 151–2.

34. Ibid., p. 152.

35. Harding, *Whose Science?,* p. 295.

36. Ibid., pp. 268ff.

37. Hall, *Lighten Our Darkness,* p. 151.

38. Minnich, *Transforming Knowledge,* pp. 32–33. I am reminded here, perhaps not so curiously, of Luther's words about the "wisdom of the saints," quoted at the end of the Preface: "For it is the wisdom of the saints to believe in the truth in opposition to the lie, in the hidden truth in opposition to the manifest truth, and in hope in opposition to hope."

39. Haraway, *Simians, Cyborgs, and Women,* p. 113.

40. Lisa M. Heldke and Stephen H. Kellert, in redefining objectivity as responsibility, make the point that "objectivity [as responsibility] requires expanding the network of responsibilities encompassed within the inquiry context. [This means, among other things] . . . to improve upon a given project by actively seeking additional observations, concerns, and other resources . . . . To improve the objectivity of inquiry, efforts at expanding responsibilities should be directed towards seeking out the perspectives of those traditionally excluded from the process by virtue of their race, ethnicity, class, gender, etc." (pp. 368, 369). See their "Objectivity as Responsibility," *Metaphilosophy* 26, no. 4 (October 1995).

41. Haraway, *Simians, Cyborgs, and Women,* p. 201.

42. Juan Luis Segundo, *The Liberation of Theology*, trans. John Drury (Maryknoll, N.Y.: Orbis Books, 1976), p. 10.

43. Again, see Heldke and Kellert's "Objectivity as Responsibility," where "to develop good knowledge," inquirers are obligated "to respond, to be answerable to others' demands, criticisms and constraints," and they "may be held to account for their practices" (pp. 363, 364).

44. Patricia Hill Collins' criteria for an Afrocentric feminist epistemology include the use of dialogue (not adversarial debate) in assessing knowledge claims. Hill quotes bell hooks as observing that dialogue involves and assumes the participation of two *subjects*, not a subject and an object. See Collins' *Black Feminist Thought*, p. 212.

45. Sobrino, *The True Church and the Poor*, p. 15.

46. Ibid., p. 18.

47. Hall, whose window looks out on a vista very different from Sobrino's, nonetheless sounds a quite similar note in his characterization of the theology of the cross: "The comprehension of reality, though in itself entailing an act of unusual intellectual courage, could never satisfy a theology whose object, i.e., whose living subject, is a God intensely committed to creation, for whom the fate of the earth is a matter of parentlike yearning. Such a theology is bound always to move from theology to ethic . . . comprehension to transformation" (*Thinking the Faith*, p. 32).

48. Haraway, *Simians, Cyborgs, and Women*, p. 191.

49. *WA* 1, 138, 13ff.

50. This is my translation of a quotation taken from a Rosa Luxemburg poster that I purchased some years ago at a Green Party office in Tübingen, Germany: "Wie Lasalle sagte, ist und bleibt die revolutionärste Tat, immer das laut zu sagen, was ist." According to the poster, the quotation can be found in "In revolutionärer Stunde—'Was weiter?',", *Gesammelte Werke*, vol. 2, p. 36.

51. Harrison, *Making the Connections*, p. 249.

52. Hall, *Lighten Our Darkness*, pp. 39–40.

53. Harrison, *Making the Connections*, p. 247.

54. Hall, *Lighten Our Darkness*, p. 111.

55. Psychiatrist Walter Reich writes, "During the last five decades, many writers have tried to make sense of the Holocaust.... [But] the misbegotten efforts ... have too often yielded not understanding but rather a diminished appreciation of the intensity of history's most fiercely inhuman episode and of the extent of modern civilization's extraordinary potential for evil." See "In the Maw of the Death Machine" [a review of *Admitting the Holocaust: Collected Essays* by Lawrence L. Langer and *Art from the Ashes: A Holocaust Anthology*, ed. Lawrence L. Langer], *The New York Times Book Review*, 29 (January 1995): 1, 25–26.

56. See especially Herman, *Trauma and Recovery*.

57. Ernest Becker's *The Denial of Death* (New York: Free Press, 1973) is only one of the best and best-known works to deal this profound theme. It is interesting to reflect on why several reviewers would have used the word "brave" to describe Becker's treatment.

58. A song on the album *Sweet Honey in the Rock Live at Carnegie Hall* begins by describing clothing "touched by hands from all over the world," made of cotton grown in a Salvadoran province "soaked in blood," and ends with the question that is also the song's title, "Are My Hands Clean?" The liner notes indicate that the lyrics (© 1985 Songtalk Publishing Co.) are based on an article written by John Cavanaugh, an Institute for Policy Studies fellow, entitled "The Journey of a Blouse: A Global Assembly."

59. Grace Janzten, "Epistemology, Religious Experience, and Religious Belief," p. 281.

60. Harding, *Whose Science?*, p. 169.

61. Hall, *Lighten Our Darkness*, p. 116.

62. Ibid., p. 205.

63. Elizabeth A. Johnson, *She Who Is: The Mystery of God in Feminist Theological Discourse* (New York: Crossroad, 1992), p. 63.

64. *LW,* vol. 31, p. 41.

65. Alice Walker, *Possessing the Secret of Joy* (New York: Pocket Books, 1992), p. 165.

66. A line from a Peter, Paul, and Mary song entitled "El Salvador," written by Noel Paul Stookey and Jim Wallis (© 1983 Neworld Media Music [ASCAP]). The song is on the Peter, Paul, and Mary album *No Easy Walk to Freedom.*

67. Harding, *Whose Science?,* p. 216.

68. Sobrino, *Christology at the Crossroads,* p. 214, 215.

69. Ibid., pp. 220–1.

70. Welch, *Communities of Resistance,* p. 89.

71. Haraway, *Simians, Cyborgs, and Women,* p. 192.

72. Miles emphasizes the importance of Luther's "revolutionary insight concerning the location of the event of justification in 'the bottom of the heart'" (Miles, "The Rope Breaks," p. 239), what is also referred to in Latin (*sententia/conscientia*) and German (*Gewissen*) texts of the Lectures on Jonah (*LW,* vol. 19) as "conscience." She argues that "'consciousness' is . . . more accurate [than 'conscience'] in denoting Luther's meaning in [our] contemporary usage. 'Conscience' carries connotations that emphasize a socially conditioned sense of guilt, while 'consciousness' designates a subjective activity in which thinking and feeling are coordinated in the construction of a world view and self-image that govern, in turn, the formation of one's perceptions, values, and behavior. Luther's description of the capacity of the justification event to constellate altered and more accurate values, perceptions, and emotions is better described by 'consciousness' than by 'conscience'" (p. 239n).

73. Sobrino, *Christology at the Crossroads,* pp. 222–3.

74. Fiddes, *Past Event,* p. 199.

75. Harrison, *Making the Connections,* p. 244.

76. There is no excuse, here or elsewhere, for asking women in particular—or any marginalized people whose problem has been self-suppression rather than self-assertion over others—to "disown themselves" or "divest themselves of ego." Elizabeth Johnson uses these expressions in her discussion of the classical theological notions of conversion (Johnson, *She Who Is,* pp. 62ff); they work well here, too.

77. Carter Heyward, *Our Passion for Justice: Images of Power, Sexuality, and Liberation* (New York: Pilgrim Press, 1984), p. 207.

78. Dietrich Bonhoeffer, *Letters and Papers from Prison,* ed. Eberhard Bethge (New York: Macmillan Publishing Co., 1971), p. 300.

79. Ibid.

80. See, for example, Gustavo Gutiérrez' *On Job: God-Talk and the Suffering of the Innocent,* trans. Matthew J. O'Connell (Maryknoll, N.Y.: Orbis Books, 1987), pp. xiiif.

81. Harding, "The Instability of Analytical Categories," p. 649.

82. Welch, *Communities of Resistance,* p. 78.

83. Phil. 1:9–10.

Chapter 4

1. The qualifier "privileged" is used here deliberately. There are some churches today, and have been some throughout the history of the Christian movement, that have not exercised privilege or wielded power, locally or globally; some have refused to do so, while others have been unable to, for one reason or another. My experience with the Salvadoran Lutheran church and my knowledge of others that work and worship in extremis has brought this home to me in an unmistakable way. This objection refers to a privileged, not a persecuted, church.

2. Delores S. Williams, *Sisters in the Wilderness: The Challenge of Womanist God-Talk* (Maryknoll, N.Y.: Orbis Books, 1993), p. 162. Williams briefly describes key historical atonement theories since Origen. Her book deals among other themes with surrogacy (which she argues is the basis for the unique character of black women's oppression), and makes a convincing historical and theological case that black women's salvation does not depend on any form of surrogacy human understandings of God may have sacralized.

A helpful short historical summary of images and concepts of atonement appears in the first chapter of Fiddes' *Past Event and Present Salvation*, where he makes the following observation: "The sheer variety of images and concepts for atonement is . . . evidence that Christian faith *has* found that the event of the cross touches life at many points. The church has failed to exhaust the meaning of the cross because it makes contact with a human need which is many-dimensional. . . . The cultural conditioning of the theology can . . . have the positive effect of *locating* where the 'mystery in our midst' is to be found" (p. 5).

3. Elisabeth Schüssler Fiorenza, *Jesus: Miriam's Child, Sophia's Prophet: Critical Issues in Feminist Christology* (New York: Continuum, 1994), p. 107. Schüssler Fiorenza's chapter entitled "Proclaimed by Women: The Execution of Jesus and the Theology of the Cross" contains a lucid and succinct summary of feminist critiques of the theology of the cross (though not Luther's specifically), replete with references to most of the best such critiques. (To her reference to Elisabeth Moltmann-Wendel, I would add another—which itself lifts up Schüssler Fiorenza's work on this issue—namely, Moltmann-Wendel's "Is There a Feminist Theology of the Cross?" in *The Scandal of a Crucified World: Perspectives on the Cross and Suffering*, ed. Yacob Tesfai [Maryknoll, N.Y.: Orbis Books, 1994], pp. 87–98. Hereafter referred to as *The Scandal*, ed. Tesfai.) The works Schüssler Fiorenza refers to, in turn, contain a host of other worthwhile references to

both feminist and traditional treatments of atonement theories and the theology of the cross.

4. Fiddes, *Past Event,* p. 32.

5. Simon E. Maimela, "The Suffering of Human Divisions and the Cross," in *The Scandal,* ed. Tesfai, p. 37. The essays in this volume resulted from a 1992 consultation sponsored by the Institute for Ecumenical Research (Strasbourg, France). The editor, Yacob Tesfai, writes that it "focused mostly on Third World understandings of the cross and suffering, with an opening to dialogue with others who have similar concerns. . . . [Our] guiding concern . . . [was] to address the division and unity of humanity in the face of suffering" (p. vii). The absence of African, Asian, and Latin American feminist women's voices at this consultation (at least in this published account) is remarkable; the single (and very good) feminist contribution, which is also the only one written by a woman, is by a European. References to the issue/problem of sexism (in general, and specifically in theological circles) or to the suffering of women and children, so often justified by reference to the "self-sacrifice" of Jesus on the cross, are few and in passing. We all have a long way to go in drawing the full implications of privilege and suffering in light of the cross!

6. von Loewenich, *Luther's Theology of the Cross,* p. 18. It is interesting to note that von Loewenich first made this comment in the original (German) edition of his book, published in 1929, and saw no reason to modify it in the 1976 translation from which it is quoted here. This is the same theologian who underscored the "eminently practical" character of Luther's theology of the cross: "It is distinguished from the theology of glory precisely because it leads a person out of his spectator stance . . . . If we are serious about . . . the theology of the cross, we are faced with the demand of a life under the cross" (pp. 112, 113).

7. Jean-Marc Éla, "The Memory of the African People and the Cross of Christ," in *The Scandal,* ed. Tesfai, p. 33.

8. Jürgen Moltmann observes that "[t]he church has much abused the theology of the cross . . . in the interest of those who cause the suffering. Too often, peasants, Indians and black slaves have been called upon by the representatives of the dominant religion to accept their sufferings as 'their cross' and not to rebel against them. Luther need not have recommended the peasants to accept their suffering as their cross. They already bore the burdens their masters imposed on them. Instead, a sermon on the cross would have done [those] . . . who ruled them a great deal of good, if it was aimed at setting them free from their pride and moving them to an attitude of solidarity with their victims. Thus it makes a difference who speaks . . . ." See Jürgen Moltmann, *The Crucified God: The Cross of Christ as the Foundation and Criticism of Christian Theology*, trans. R. A. Wilson and John Bowden (Minneapolis: Fortress Press, 1993), p. 49.

9. Like the German Augustinian, the Spanish Dominican was a faithful son and servant of the Holy Roman Church. Both began by unintentionally but unmistakably threatening the powerful, and both drew theological and political reprisals. Neither was willing to recant. It would be fascinating to pursue and reflect on these and other comparisons, as well as the real contrasts, between Luther and de las Casas. For a brief account of those who, like de las Casas, experienced conversion to the oppressed in the "New World," see Maximiliano Salinas, "The Voices of Those Who Spoke up for the Victims," in *1492–1992: The Voice of the Victims*, ed. Leonardo Boff and Virgil Elizondo (London: SCM Press, 1990), pp. 101–9.

10. Andreas A. Yewangoe, "An Asian Perspective on the Cross and Suffering," in *The Scandal*, ed. Tesfai, p. 62.

11. C. S. Song, "Christian Mission Toward Abolition of the Cross," in *The Scandal*, ed. Tesfai, p. 141.

12. James H. Cone, "An African-American Perspective on the Cross and Suffering," in *The Scandal*, ed. Tesfai, p. 58.

13. Hall, *Lighten Our Darkness,* pp. 187–88.
14. Maimela, in *The Scandal,* ed. Tesfai, p. 37.
15. Éla, in *The Scandal,* ed. Tesfai, pp. 18, 22.
16. Joanne Carlson Brown and Carole R. Bohn, "For God So Loved the World?" In *Christianity, Patriarchy, and Abuse: A Feminist Critique,* ed. Joanne Carlson Brown and Carole R. Bohn (Cleveland: Pilgrim Press, 1989), p. 2. This opening essay is a trenchant and powerful critique of the centrality of the cross/atonement in Christianity.
17. Hall, *Lighten Our Darkness,* p. 204.
18. Fiddes, *Past Event,* p. 196.
19. Hall, *Lighten Our Darkness,* pp. 140, 141. Hall reminds us of the "bland, sweetly Aryan Jesus who can never be dissociated now from that picture by Sallman, Christ-of-the-chestnut-hair, which can be found in literally every town, village, and city on this continent" (p. 141). It is hard to overestimate the number of boy and girl children of every color who, having incorporated just *that* visual image of Jesus, come to "know" with certainty that Jesus is a white man.
20. Ibid.
21. Tesfai, in *The Scandal,* ed. Tesfai, p. 7. Emphasis added.
22. Ibid., p. 13.
23. Altmann, "A Latin American Perspective on the Cross and Suffering," in *The Scandal,* ed. Tesfai, p. 84.
24. But see Fiddes, *Past Event,* p. 215: " . . . [T]he Christ who 'offered up prayers with strong cries and tears' could hardly be misconstrued as giving thanks for the cross." No more than could Jesus' soul-wrenching cry, "My God, my God, why have you forsaken me?"
25. von Loewenich discusses Luther's understanding of suffering as part of "Life under the Cross," pp. 112ff; his reflections are cogent, spare, and replete with references to Luther's works. (See von Loewenich, *Luther's Theology of the Cross.*)

26. Ibid., p. 113.

27. See von Loewenich, *Luther's Theology of the Cross,* p. 122, where the author directs the reader's attention to various Luther texts that clarify content and context for Luther's disapproval of suffering aimed to curry favor with God. "In the theology of the cross," von Loewenich writes, "suffering is understood throughout theologically, not anthropologically, that is, *not on the basis of reflection on human nature,* but on the basis of God's revelatory activity *in history.* And the fact that this revelation of God is summed up on the cross explains the high significance of the idea of suffering" (pp. 119–20, emphasis added).

28. Ibid., p. 123.

29. For example, the internal struggle he characterized as *Anfechtung;* the mortal threat to his life that the pope's bull of excommunication carried with it.

30. Sölle, *Suffering,* p. 88.

31. In an article titled "Medicine and the Question of Suffering," Richard B. Gunderman argues that medical training and medicine as a profession are little concerned with suffering. "Knowingly to choose a career in medicine," he writes, "requires courage, and so, too, does caring for patients. To care for the patient means opening oneself up to the reality of suffering, and thereby to the possibility of suffering oneself" (Guderman, "Medicine and the Question of Suffering," *Second Opinion* 14 [July 1990]: 24). His insight has applications beyond his own professional venue.

32. Sölle, *Suffering,* p. 70.

33. Sobrino, *The True Church and the Poor,* p. 29.

34. Welch, *Communities of Resistance,* p. 89.

35. Ibid.

36. Elizabeth Bettenhausen, foreword to *Christianity, Patriarchy, and Abuse,* ed. Joanne Carlson Brown and Carol R. Bohn, p. xii.

37. Bonhoeffer, *Letters and Papers,* p. 17.

38. Ibid., pp. 16, 17.

39. Rebecca Chopp, *The Praxis of Suffering: An Interpretation of Liberation and Political Theologies* (Maryknoll, N.Y.: Orbis Books, 1986), p. 120.
40. Siirala, *Divine Humanness*, pp. 100–1.
41. Sölle, *Suffering*, p. 177.

Conclusion

1. Sölle, *Suffering*, p. 3.
2. Herman, *Trauma and Recovery*, p. 122.
3. In this connection, see Heldke and Kellert, who argue that "a commitment to responsibility *works* . . . to promote objectivity" through "three overlapping tasks," the first of which is "acknowledging" responsibility: ". . . [T]hose in the inquiry context [must] recognize and accept their positions in that context . . . . This requirement entails recognizing the demands made by others in the inquiry context, for these demands cannot be met adequately if their very existence is denied. Objectivity will suffer under attempts to deny the fact that relationships . . . constitute the inquiry context" (p. 367). It seems to me that these observations are particularly apt in the "inquiry context" Herman is describing. (See Heldke and Kellert, "Objectivity as Responsibility.")
4. Herman, *Trauma and Recovery*, p. 178.
5. Ibid., p. 154.
6. Ibid., p. 7.
7. Ibid., p. 145.
8. Ibid., p. 144.
9. Ibid., p. 181.
10. Herman's work in this area offers an orientation to the study of trauma and the treatment of survivors that I have benefited from, not only as the author of this book but also as a social worker. I assume full responsibility for my interpretation of her work in terms of an epistemology of the cross.

11. Polanyi, *Personal Knowledge*, p. 256. Although Polanyi does not use the word theologically, it can certainly call up theological connotations, here or elsewhere.

12. Minnich makes this pithy comment: "What we need to comprehend is and will be related to what we need to do; what we need to do is related to what we need to comprehend" (Minnich, *Transforming Knowledge*, p. 184).

13. J. Louis Martyn, "Epistemology at the Turn of the Ages: 2 Corinthians 5:16," *Christian History and Interpretation: Studies Presented to John Knox*, ed. W. R. Farmer, C. F. D. Moule, and R. R. Niebuhr (Cambridge: At the University Press, 1967), p. 286. Martyn's wonderful exegesis underscores the inextricable, reciprocal relationship between how one knows and how one lives. Martyn interprets Paul as telling the Corinthians that " . . . the implied opposite of knowing *kata sarka* [according to the flesh] is not knowing *kata pneuma* [according to the spirit] but rather knowing *kata stauron* . . . . The essential failure of the Corinthians consists in their inflexible determination to live either *before* the cross [legalistically] . . . or *after* the cross [triumphalistically] . . . rather than *in* the cross." The living and knowing to which Paul refers occur in the world, here and now, and have as much to do with science, ethics, politics, and theology as with justification and knowledge of God.

14. Harding, *Whose Science?*, p. 102.

Bibliography

Althaus, Paul. *The Ethics of Martin Luther.* Translated by Robert C. Schultz. Philadelphia: Fortress Press, 1972.

————. *The Theology of Martin Luther.* Translated by Robert C. Schultz. Philadelphia: Fortress Press, 1966.

Altmann, Walter. *Luther and Liberation: A Latin American Perspective.* Translated by Mary M. Solberg. Minneapolis: Fortress Press, 1992.

Antony, Louise M., and Charlotte Witt, eds. *A Mind of One's Own: Feminist Essays on Reason and Objectivity.* New York: Westview Press, 1994.

Assmann, Hugo. "Statement by Hugo Assmann." In *Theology in the Americas,* edited by Sergio Torres and John Eagleson. Maryknoll, N.Y.: Orbis Books, 1976.

Becker, Ernest. *The Denial of Death.* New York: Free Press, 1973.

Bettenhausen, Elizabeth. "Dependence, Liberation, and Justification." *Word & World* 7, no. 1 (Winter 1987): 59–69.

Bonhoeffer, Dietrich. *Letters and Papers from Prison.* Enl. ed. Edited by Eberhard Bethge. New York: Macmillan Publishing Company, 1971.

Bordo, Susan. "The Cartesian Masculinization of Thought." *Signs* 11, no. 3 (1986): 439–56.

Brecht, Martin. *Martin Luther: His Road to Reformation 1483–1521.* Translated by James L. Schaaf. Philadelphia: Fortress Press, 1985.

Briggs, Sheila M. "The Politics of Identity and the Politics of Interpretation." *Union Seminary Quarterly Review* 43, no. 1 (1989): 163–80.

√ Brown, Joanne Carlson, and Carol R. Bohn, eds. *Christianity, Patriarchy, and Abuse: A Feminist Critique.* Cleveland: Pilgrim Press, 1989.

Chadwick, Owen. *The Reformation.* New York: Penguin Books, 1964, 1972.

Chopp, Rebecca. *The Praxis of Suffering: An Interpretation of Liberation and Political Theologies.* Maryknoll, N.Y.: Orbis Books, 1986.

Chung Hyun Kyung. *Struggle to Be the Sun Again: Introducing Asian Women's Theology.* Maryknoll, N.Y.: Orbis Books, 1990.

Code, Lorraine. *What Can She Know? Feminist Theory and the Construction of Knowledge.* Ithaca, N.Y.: Cornell University Press, 1991.

Collins, Patricia Hill. *Black Feminist Thought: Knowledge, Consciousness, and the Politics of Empowerment.* New York: Routledge, 1991.

————. "Learning from the Outsider Within: The Sociological Significance of Black Feminist Thought." *Social Problems* 33, no. 6 (1986).

Cone, James H. *God of the Oppressed.* New York: Seabury Press, 1975.

Cousar, Charles B. *A Theology of the Cross: The Death of Jesus in the Pauline Letters.* Minneapolis: Fortress Press, 1990.

D. Martin Luthers Werke: Kritische Gesamtausgabe. Weimar: Hermann Böhlaus Nachfolger, 1883–.

Dillenberger, John, ed. *Martin Luther: Selections from His Writings.* Garden City, N.Y.: Anchor Books, 1961.

Ebeling, Gerhard. *Luther: An Introduction to His Thought.* Translated by R. A. Wilson. Philadelphia: Fortress Press, 1970.

Elshout, Elly, et al. "Women with Disabilities: A Challenge to Feminist Theology," *Journal of Feminist Studies in Religion* 10, no. 2 (1994): 99–134.

Erikson, Erik H. *Young Man Luther: A Study in Psychoanalysis and History*. New York: W. W. Norton, 1958.

Fiddes, Paul S. *Past Event and Present Salvation: The Christian Idea of Atonement*. Louisville, Ky.: Westminster/John Knox Press, 1989.

Fulkerson, Mary McClintock. *Changing the Subject: Women's Discourses and Feminist Theology*. Minneapolis: Fortress Press, 1994.

Gerrish, Brian. *Grace and Reason: A Study in the Theology of Luther*. Oxford: At the Clarendon Press, 1962.

Gunderman, Richard B. "Medicine and the Question of Suffering." *Second Opinion* 14 (July 1990): 15–25.

Gutiérrez, Gustavo. *On Job: God-Talk and the Suffering of the Innocent*. Translated by Matthew J. O'Connell. Maryknoll, N.Y.: Orbis Books, 1987.

Hall, Douglas John. *Lighten Our Darkness: Toward an Indigenous Theology of the Cross*. Philadelphia: Westminster Press, 1976.

————. *Thinking the Faith: Christian Theology in a North American Context*. Minneapolis: Augsburg Publishing House, 1989.

Hanks, Tomás. "El testimonio evangélico a los pobres y oprimidos." *Vida y Pensamiento* 4, nos. 1–2 (1984): 21–42.

Haraway, Donna. *Simians, Cyborgs, and Women: The Reinvention of Nature*. New York: Routledge, 1991.

Harding, Sandra. "The Instability of Analytical Categories in Feminist Theory." *Signs* 11, no. 4 (1986): 645–64.

————. *The Science Question in Feminism*. Ithaca, N.Y.: Cornell University Press, 1986.

————. *Whose Science? Whose Knowledge? Thinking from Women's Lives*. Ithaca, N.Y.: Cornell University Press, 1991.

Harran, Marilyn J. *Luther on Conversion: The Early Years.* Ithaca, N.Y.: Cornell University Press, 1983.

Harrison, Beverly Wildung. *Making the Connections: Essays in Feminist Social Ethics.* Edited by Carol S. Robb. Boston: Beacon Press, 1985.

Hartsock, Nancy C. M. *Money, Sex, and Power: Toward a Feminist Historical Materialism.* Boston: Northeastern University Press, 1983.

Heldke, Lisa M., and Stephen H. Kellert. "Objectivity as Responsibility." *Metaphilosophy* 26, no. 4 (October 1995): 360–78.

Herman, Judith Lewis. *Trauma and Recovery.* New York: Basic Books, 1992.

Heyward, Carter. *Our Passion for Justice: Images of Power, Sexuality, and Liberation.* New York: Pilgrim Press, 1984.

hooks, bell [Gloria Watkins]. "Choosing the Margin as a Space of Radical Openness." In *Yearning: Race, Gender, and Cultural Politics.* Boston: South End Press, 1990.

Hordern, William. *Experience and Faith: The Significance of Luther for Understanding Today's Experiential Religion.* Minneapolis: Augsburg Publishing House, 1983.

Jaggar, Alison M. "Feminist Ethics: Projects, Problems, Prospects." In *Feminist Ethics,* edited by Claudia Card. Lawrence: University Press of Kansas, 1991.

———. "Feminist Politics and Epistemology: Justifying Feminist Theory." In *Feminist Politics and Human Nature.* Totowa, N.J.: Rowman & Allenheld, 1983.

Jantzen, Grace. "Epistemology, Religious Experience, and Religious Belief." *Modern Theology* 3, no. 4 (1987): 277–291.

Johnson, Elizabeth A. *She Who Is: The Mystery of God in Feminist Theological Discourse.* New York: Crossroad, 1992.

Jordan, June. *On Call: Political Essays.* Boston: South End Press, 1985.

Keller, Evelyn Fox. *Reflections on Gender and Science*. New Haven, Conn.: Yale University Press, 1985.

Lehmann, Paul L. *The Decalogue and a Human Future: The Meaning of the Commandments for Making and Keeping Human Life Human*. Grand Rapids, Mich.: William B. Eerdmans Publishing, 1995.

Loeschen, John R. *Wrestling with Luther: An Introduction to the Study of His Thought*. St. Louis, Mo.: Concordia Publishing House, 1976.

Loewenich, Walther von. *Luther's Theology of the Cross*. Translated by Herbert J. A. Bouman. Belfast: Christian Journals, 1976.

Lugones, Maria. "On the Logic of Pluralist Feminism." In *Feminist Ethics*, edited by Claudia Card. Lawrence: University Press of Kansas, 1991.

Luther, Martin. *Luther: Early Theological Works*. Vol. 16. Library of Christian Classics. Edited and translated by James Atkinson. Philadelphia: Westminster Press, 1962.

Luther, Martin. *Luther: Lectures on Romans*. Edited by Wilhelm Pauck. Philadelphia: Westminster Press, 1961.

Luther, Martin. *Luther's Works*. 55 vols. Edited by Jaroslav Pelikan and Helmut T. Lehmann. St. Louis: Concordia Publishing House, and Philadelphia: Fortress Press, 1955–.

Mahowald, Mary B. "On Treatment of Myopia: Feminist Standpoint Theory and Bioethics." In *Feminism & Bioethics: Beyond Reproduction*, edited by Susan D. Wolf. New York: Oxford University Press, 1996.

Martyn, J. Louis. "Epistemology at the Turn of the Ages: 2 Corinthians 5:16." In *Christian History and Interpretation: Studies Presented to John Knox*, edited by W. R. Farmer, C. F. D. Moule, and R. R. Niebuhr. Cambridge: At the University Press, 1967.

McGrath, Alister E. *Luther's Theology of the Cross*. Oxford: Basil Blackwell, 1985.

Miles, Margaret R. "'The Rope Breaks When It Is Tightest': Luther on the Body, Consciousness, and the Word."

Harvard Theological Review 77, nos. 3–4 (1984): 239–258.

Minnich, Elizabeth Kamarck. "Resisting Reality: Critique and Creativity." *Spotlight on Teaching* 2, no. 2 (1994): 1–5.

————. *Transforming Knowledge.* Philadelphia: Temple University Press, 1990.

Moltmann, Jürgen. *The Crucified God: The Cross of Christ as the Foundation and Criticism of Christian Theology.* Translated by R.A. Wilson and John Bowden. Minneapolis: Fortress Press, 1993.

Morse, Christopher. *Not Every Spirit: A Dogmatics of Christian Disbelief.* Valley Forge, Penn.: Trinity Press International, 1994.

Nussbaum, Martha. "Feminists and Philosophy." Review of *A Mind of One's Own: Feminist Essays on Reason and Objectivity*, edited by Louise M. Antony and Charlotte Witt. *The New York Review of Books* 41, no. 17 (20 October 1994): 59–63.

Pellauer, Mary D. "Feminist Theology: Challenges and Consolations for Lutherans." *dialog* 24, no. 1 (Winter 1985): 19–25.

Polanyi, Michael. *Personal Knowledge: Towards a Post-Critical Philosophy.* Chicago: University of Chicago Press, 1958, 1962.

Rankin, William. "The Moral Use of Knowledge: Part 2." *Plumbline* 11, no. 1 (April 1983): 4–12.

Reich, Walter. "In the Maw of the Death Machine." Review of *Admitting the Holocaust: Collected Essays*, by Lawrence L. Langer and *Art from the Ashes: A Holocaust Anthology*, edited by Lawrence L. Langer. *New York Times Book Review.* 29 January 1995.

Rorty, Richard. *Philosophy and the Mirror of Nature.* Princeton, N.J.: Princeton University Press, 1979.

Rose, Hilary. "Hand, Brain, and Heart: A Feminist Epistemology for the Natural Sciences." *Signs* 9, no. 1 (1983): 73–90.

Rosser, Sue V. *Teaching Science and Health from a Feminist Perspective.* New York: Pergamon Press, 1986.

Ruddick, Sara. *Maternal Thinking: Toward a Politics of Peace.* Boston: Beacon Press, 1989.

Salinas, Maximiliano. "The Voices of Those Who Spoke up for the Victims." In *1492–1992: The Voice of the Victims.* Edited by Leonardo Boff and Victor Elizondo. A Concilium Special. London: SCM Press, 1990.

Schüssler Fiorenza, Elisabeth. *Jesus: Miriam's Child, Sophia's Prophet: Critical Issues in Feminist Christology.* New York: Continuum, 1994.

Segundo, Juan Luis. *The Liberation of Theology.* Translated by John Drury. Maryknoll, N.Y.: Orbis Books, 1976.

Sherwin, Susan. *No Longer Patient: Feminist Ethics and Health Care.* Philadelphia: Temple University Press, 1992.

Siirala, Aarne. *Divine Humanness.* Translated by T. A. Kantonen. Philadelphia: Fortress Press, 1970.

Sittler, Joseph. *Gravity and Grace: Reflections and Provocations.* Edited by Linda-Marie Delloff. Minneapolis: Augsburg Publishing House, 1986.

Sobrino, Jon. *Christology at the Crossroads.* Translated by John Drury. Maryknoll, N.Y.: Orbis Books, 1978.

———. *The True Church and the Poor.* Translated by Matthew J. O'Donnell. Maryknoll, N.Y.: Orbis Books, 1984.

Sobrino, Jon, and Juan Hernández Pico. *Theology of Christian Solidarity.* Translated by Phillip Berryman. Maryknoll, N.Y.: Orbis Books, 1985.

Sölle, Dorothee. *Suffering.* Translated by Everett R. Kalin. Philadelphia: Fortress Press, 1975.

Tappert, Theodore G., ed. and trans. *The Book of Concord.* Philadelphia: Fortress Press, 1959.

Tesfai, Yacob, ed. *The Scandal of a Crucified World: Perspectives on the Cross and Suffering.* Maryknoll, N.Y.: Orbis Books, 1994.

Vercruysse, Joseph E. "Luther's Theology of the Cross at the Time of the Heidelberg Disputation." *Gregorianum* 57 (1976): 523–48.

Walker, Alice. *Possessing the Secret of Joy.* New York: Pocket Books, 1992.

Walker, Margaret Urban. "Moral Understandings: Alternative 'Epistemology' for Feminist Ethics." In *Explorations in Feminist Ethics: Theory and Practice,* edited by Eve Browning Cole and Susan Coultrap-McQuin. Bloomington: Indiana University Press, 1992.

Welch, Sharon D. *Communities of Resistance and Solidarity: A Feminist Theology of Liberation.* Maryknoll, N.Y.: Orbis Books, 1985.

Wetherilt, Ann Kirkus. *That They May Be Many: Voices of Women, Echoes of God.* New York: Continuum, 1994.

Williams, Delores S. *Sisters in the Wilderness: The Challenge of Womanist God-Talk.* Maryknoll, N.Y.: Orbis Books, 1993.

Index

add chapter 3 to Frei
read ch. 4. - Role Play.

- Not a feminist theology
but a feminist epistemology.

- righteousness by faith is communal not individual.
- Solberg's suffering is greater than self.
  Is it through observing or living among in which
  we understand suffering.